IN THE HEART OF THE SEAS

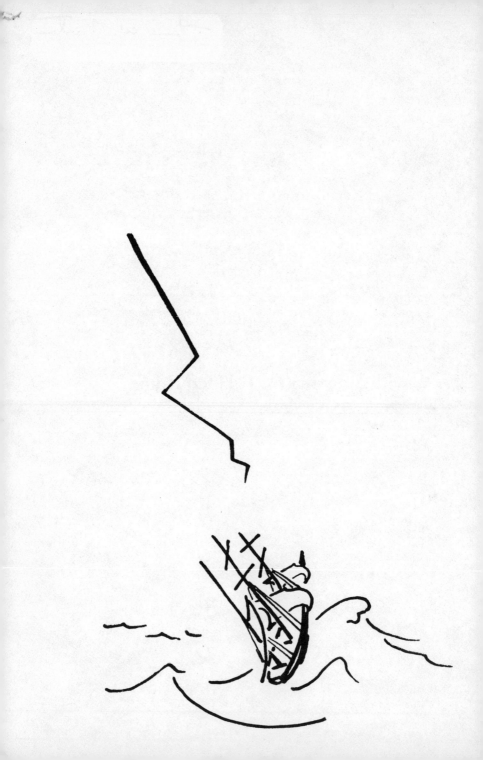

IN THE HEART OF THE SEAS
THE SEAS   A Story of a
Journey to the Land of Israel by
Shmuel Yosef Agnon, translated
from the Hebrew by I. M. Lask,
with drawings by T. Herzl Rome

SCHOCKEN BOOKS • NEW YORK

Start in Poland

i

Dust
of
the roads

JUST before the first of the hasidim went up to the Land of Israel, a certain man named Hananiah found his way to their House of Study. His clothes were torn, rags were wound around his legs, and he wore no boots on his feet; his hair and beard were covered with the dust of the roads, and all his worldly goods were tied up in a little bundle which he carried with him in his kerchief.

Ye sons of the living God, said Hananiah to the comrades, I have heard that you are about to go up to the Land of Israel. I beg you to inscribe me in your register.

He Who will bring us up to the Land, said they to him, will bring you up as well. And they wrote his name in their list and assigned him a place to rest in the House of Study. He rejoiced in them because he would go up to the Land of Israel with them; while they rejoiced in him because he would complete the quorum, and they could pray as a congregation on their journey.

It can clearly be seen, said the comrades to Hananiah, that you have walked far.

True indeed, said he to them. It is not a short distance I have come.

Where were you? they asked.

Where was I? he answered. And where was I not?

Whereupon they began to question him on every side, until at last he recounted all his travels.

At first, said Hananiah, I went from my town to another town, and from that town to yet another. In that

7

way I went from place to place until I reached the frontier of a country where no man is permitted to pass unless he pays a tax to the king. They took my money from me and stripped me naked, and left me nothing but a kerchief with which to cover myself. But the people of that town took pity on me, and clothed me and gave me all I needed, a prayer shawl and phylacteries and a fringed garment.

Now in that country it is cold for the greater part of the year. At the Feast of Weeks their houses stand in snow though it is May, while at the Feast of Booths a man cannot even hold the *lulav* to shake it on account of the cold; and they have no citrons for the blessing. So what they do is, all the congregations share a single citron, a slice for each congregation. They hallow the Sabbath over black bread instead of white wheaten loaves, and they mark the Sabbath's end by drinking milk, for they have no wine. When I told them where I was going, they took me for an exaggerator, because they had never in all their days heard of any man who really and truly went up to the Land of Israel.

By that time I myself was beginning to doubt whether the Land of Israel actually existed; so I decided I had better leave them to themselves and went away. Better, said I to myself, that I should perish on the way and not lose my faith in the Land of Israel.

I do not remember how long a time I had been journeying or the places to which I came, but at length I reached a robbers' den. The robbers allowed me to stay among them and did not do anything to me; but every time they went off on their business they would say to me, Pray on our behalf that we may not be caught. And

8

most of them had their good qualities, and were merciful, and were a stay and prop to the poor in their need, and believed in the Creator; and once they took an oath by the Everlasting they would never go back on their word even if they were to lose their lives. And they were not robbers to begin with, but lords and nobles whose oppressors compelled them to give up their fields; and so they came to try their hands at robbery and pillage.

One of them I saw putting on phylacteries. I made the mistake of thinking that he was a Jew, though he was not one; but the robber chief before him had worn phylacteries, and when he was killed, his successor put them on.

Now this was the story of how that robber chief of theirs had been killed. He used to leave his booty with a certain Greek priest. But once the priest denied that anything had been left with him. The robber chief threatened to take vengeance on him; whereupon the priest went and denounced him to the king; the king at once ordered him to be killed.

When they took the robber chief off to be executed, they said to him, If you tell us where your comrades are, we shall let you go.

You do what you have to do, said he to them.

Well, they tied the rope around his neck and sent his soul on its way. When he died, he said, Alas for you, O my wife, and alas for my children, whom I leave behind to be orphans.

Once, continued Hananiah, the new robber chief wished to lead me to the Land of Israel through a certain cave. But the idea entered my heart that maybe it would not be His blessed will for a robber to be my groomsman. And since I was possessed by this idea, I did not go with him, for if it had been His blessed will that I should go with him, would He ever have let such a thought enter my mind? But I felt ashamed because I did not accept his favor, and so I went on to another country.

Now in this other country all their days are toil, so that they have neither Sabbath nor festivals; so that at last I forgot when it was the Sabbath. So whenever I went from one place to another, I never went farther than a Sabbath journey of two thousand ells for fear that that day might be a Sabbath or festival.

Once a gentleman met me on the way and said, Where are you going?

To town, I answered.

He invited me up into his carriage. When he saw that I was not getting up, he raised his voice and shouted, Shadai. Now he was speaking Polish and in Polish *shadai* means sit down, but I did not know it and thought that he was using the Holy Name of Shaddai; so up I jumped into his carriage.

It was the Day of Atonement; but I never knew it until we reached town at the time they were praying the Closing Prayer. At once I flung myself off the carriage, and took off my shoes, and entered the synagogue, and lay outstretched, and wept all that night and all of the day following. There I heard the Land of Israel being mentioned. So I gave ear and heard people telling one another how the men of Buczacz had decided to go up to the Land. At once I started off and came here to you; and since I went barefoot, my legs became swollen and it took a long time.

They went and fetched him boots, but he would not accept them. Rabbi Akiba, they reminded him, ordained seven things, and one of them was to be careful to wear shoes. To which Hananiah replied, These feet did not feel the sanctity of the Day of Atonement; let them remain bare.

After Hananiah had told all this, he untied his kerchief, took out a Book of Psalms, and read until the time arrived for the Afternoon Prayer. Following the prayer, he took a candle and went on reading. Seeing that the lamp had grown rusty, he took his kerchief and made a knot in it. Next morning, when he took out his prayer shawl and phylacteries from that kerchief, he said to himself, What is this knot for? To remember that rusty lamp.

So he took the lamp and all the other vessels for light in the House of Study, and mixed sand and water, and went and sat him down behind the stove, and rubbed them and polished them until they shone like new. That day people said, the lamps in our House of Study are worthy of lighting before Him who hath light in Zion.

And Hananiah did something else; he made little hollow dishes for the lamps; for in the lands of Edom tallow candles are lit and thrust upright into the candlestick, but in the Land of Beauty it is the custom to light oil lamps, a dish being filled with oil and the wick placed within it. Therefore Hananiah went and set dishes under the candlesticks, that they might fill them with oil.

But it was not only the illuminating vessels that Hananiah rubbed and polished. He also took the ewer and the pitcher and the holy vessels and all those vessels and implements within which the _Shekhinah,_ the Divine Presence, conceals herself; and made them all shine. He likewise repaired the torn books, setting them in fresh boards and wrapping them up in fine skins. The day before, they had been torn and sooty, but that day they rejoiced as on the day they had been given to the children of Israel on Mount Sinai.

Are you a coppersmith? Hananiah was asked.

No coppersmith am I, said he to those who asked, nor yet a bookbinder; but when I see a defective vessel, I feel pity for it and I say, This vessel seeks its completion. Then the Holy One, blessed be he, says to me, Do this or do that, and I do it.

Here is a simple man, said the comrades. Yet every word he utters teaches a virtue. Wherever such a man may wander, God will be with him.

Perhaps, one of them asked Hananiah, you know how to make a box for carrying goods?

Perhaps I do, answered he.

After all, said this man, we are going a long way and we require things for the journey. Perhaps you can make me a box or trunk.

I can try, said he.

How do you try? said the other to him.

Hananiah went out to the forest and brought lumber, and sawed it into planks which he squared and planed and joined, and made into a box and painted red, which is a good color for utensils to be.

The other men who were going up to the Land saw how fine the box was and asked Hananiah to make boxes for them as well. So out he went to the forest, brought lumber and made the same sort of boxes for them. He also made a Holy Ark for the Torah Scroll which they were going to take up to the Land of Israel. He used iron nails to join all the boxes except the Holy Ark, which he joined with wooden pegs; so that if, God forbid, they should come to magnetic mountains which draw iron from vessels, this Ark would not fall apart.

Hananiah made boxes for all the travelers, but as for himself he remained satisfied with his kerchief.

THE greater part of Adar had already passed. The clouds which had been obscuring the sun's course began to shrink, while the sun grew gradually larger. What only yesterday had been the time for the Evening Prayer became the time for Afternoon Prayer today; while yesterday's getting-up time became the time to start saying the Morning Prayer today.

The snow warmed up and began to melt, and the trees of the field grew black. One day they were black as earth; the next, they would be putting forth leaves and blossoming like the Lebanon. The pools and marshes were covered by a film, and the birds began to chirp. Every day a different kind of bird would come around and there began a cheeping on every roof. Our men of good heart started going out and asking when the road would be fit for travel; they meant the month, of course, when the road would be fit for wayfarers.

Never in all their lives had these good folk so feared death as at that particular period. How great is the sanctity of the Land of Israel though it be in ruins! And what is the body's strength even at its height? For after all, suppose a man wishes to go up to the Land of Israel and does not go up, what if his soul should suddenly depart from his body and he be left lying like a dumb stone without having gone up; what would become of all his hopes?

Those who knew enough to study the Bible sat and studied the Bible; those who knew enough to study the Mishnah sat and studied the Mishnah in order to strengthen their hearts with the study of the Torah. Throughout those days neither the sun nor the moon ever saw a single one of them sitting idle. Although they were busy selling their houses and casting up their money accounts, they nevertheless crowned their days with Torah and prayer.

The Passover festival came to an end. The sun pitched its camp in the sky, and all the water in the swamps and marshes dried up. Even the big swamps had no water in them. The roads fairly asked to be put to use, and the wagoners set out on their ways. Horses began posting from one end of the world to the other, their bells jingling as they went; and the wagoners tugged at the reins and shouted, Geeup! Whoa there!

Those who were to go up to the Land gathered together at their House of Study. In came old Rabbi Shelomo, a well-disposed *kohen* who had dealt in commerce all his life, but had finally given up the estates of this world and set his heart on going up to the Land of Israel. Rabbi Shelomo used to say, If a king is angry with his servants they ought never to go far away from him. Instead, let them stand at the king's gate and la-

ment their misfortune until he sees their distress and takes pity on them.

And then in came Rabbi Alter, the slaughterer-and-inspector, who had handed over his butcher's knife to his son-in-law; and together with him came Rabbi Alter the teacher, who was his brother-in-law's son and who had spent all his days in the tent of the Torah, studying keenly and casuistically with his students. Once while he sat studying in the tractate Ketuvot about marriage contracts, it occurred to him that after all the Land of Israel is a marriage contract between Israel and the Holy One, blessed be he; and it is an accepted principle that a man must never be without his marriage contract. Whereupon he felt that as long as he continued to dwell outside the Land he would have no rest. So he ceased his studies, and dispersed his students, and sold his house and his set of the Talmud and the commentary of Alfasi, and went and inscribed himself in the list of those who were going up to the Land.

And in came Rabbi Pesah, the warden of the House of Study, who was going to the Land with his wife Tzirel, for their benefit and advantage in the hope that the merits of the Land of Israel might give them the merit of children.

And in came Rabbi Yosef Meir, who had divorced his wife because she refused to go up to the Land of Israel. Her father had sent to him, saying, If you wish to take back my daughter and dwell with her in Buczacz as before, I shall double her dowry.

Said Rabbi Yosef Meir, I have already contracted with another bride and I cannot shame her.

And in came Rabbi Moshe, the brother of Rabbi

16

Gershon, may he rest in peace, the same Rabbi Gershon whose soul departed while he was reciting the verse, 'The King hath brought me into his chambers,' as is told elsewhere in my story, 'The Rejected One.' For love of the Land of Israel Rabbi Moshe was leaving his two daughters behind and had inscribed his name and that of his wife in the register among those who were going up to the Land.

And in came Rabbi Yehudah Mendel, one of the last of the followers of Rabbi Uriel, whose soul is treasured on high. As long as Rabbi Uriel had been alive, a bond had extended all the way to his home from the Land of Israel. Once he passed away, nothing in the whole world had any value for Rabbi Yehudah Mendel until God put it in his heart to go up to the Land of Israel.

Then in came someone else whose name we have forgotten.

And in came Leibush the butcher, whom the Land of Israel afterwards spewed forth because he spoke in its disfavor, saying, Have you ever seen a country where you can find nothing but mutton?

And in came Rabbi Shmuel Yosef, the son of Rabbi Shalom Mordekhai ha-Levi of blessed memory, who was versed in the legends of the Land of Israel, those legends in which the name of the Holy One, blessed be he, is hallowed; and when he commenced lauding the Land, people could see as it were the name of the living God engraved on the tip of his tongue.

And when they all came together, Hananiah stood at the entrance, holding in his hand the kerchief containing his prayer shawl and phylacteries and other baggage, like a man who is prepared to set off at once.

The women stood in the Women's Section, while the men were sitting in the House of Study. There was Mistress Milka the coral-seller, who had entered into a second marriage on condition that her husband go up to the Land of Israel with her, and who had received a divorce from him because he would not go; and near her Feiga, her kinswoman, the widow of Rabbi Yudel of Stri, may he rest in peace, a descendant of gentry and trustees who used to send money to the poor of the Land of Israel; and near her Hinda, the wife of Rabbi Alter the slaughterer; and near her Tzirel, the wife of Rabbi Pesah the warden; and near her Esther, the wife of Rabbi Shmuel Yosef, the son of Shalom Mordekhai ha-Levi; and near her Sarah, the wife of Rabbi Moshe, grandson of Rabbi Avigdor the president, of blessed memory; and near her Pessel, the daughter of Rabbi Shelomo ha-Kohen, who had just been widowed at that time and joined her father on the journey in order to bear her suffering in the Land of Israel.

Then up rose Rabbi Shelomo ha-Kohen to his feet, and set his two hands on the table, and bowed his head, and said to them, Why do you wish to go up to the Land of Israel? Surely you know that many sufferings come upon wayfarers besides their being pressed for food, and they fear evil beasts and robbers, particularly upon the sea.

To this our men of good heart responded, saying, We are not afraid. If we are deserving in His eyes, may he be blessed, he will fetch us to the Land of Israel; and if we are not deserving (God forfend!), then we are deserving of all the troubles that may befall us.

What Rabbi Shelomo said to the men he said to the

women as well, and as the men answered so answered they.

Whereupon Rabbi Shelomo said, Happy are ye who cleave to the Land of Israel, for the Land of Israel was created only for Israel, and none can remain in the Land of Israel save Israel. All the things I said, I said only in order to increase your reward.

Thereupon Rabbi Alter the slaughterer put his hand on the shoulder of Rabbi Alter the teacher, and Rabbi Alter the teacher put his hand on the shoulder of Rabbi Alter the slaughterer, and they began dancing and singing:

> 'Oh that the salvation of Israel were come out of Zion!
> When the Lord turneth the captivity of his people,
> Let Jacob rejoice, let Israel be glad.'

Rabbi Shmuel Yosef, the son of Rabbi Shalom Mordekhai ha-Levi asked Rabbi Moshe, Perhaps you know the tune to which your brother, Rabbi Gershon of blessed memory, sang the verse, 'The King hath brought me into his chambers'?

That tune, said he, it is not our practice to sing because my brother departed from the world therewith; but I know the tune to which he sang the verse, 'Draw me, we will run after thee.' If you wish to hear it, I shall sing it for you.

All those assembled lowered their heads, and Rabbi Moshe began singing, 'Draw me, we will run after thee.'

Then Rabbi Yosef Meir rose and said, Would that we might merit to sing the verse, 'The King hath brought me into his chambers' in Jerusalem, the holy city. Those assembled responded, Amen, and they proceeded to their homes in peace.

When they left the House of Study, the whole town was already deep in slumber. The houses lay in the secret place of night, concealed by the darkness. The moon was still hidden in the skies, and only stars lit up the summits of the mountains. Buczacz lies on a mountain, and it seemed as though the stars were bound to her rooftops. Suddenly the moon came out and lit up all the town. The river Stripa, which had previously been covered by darkness, suddenly gleamed silver, and the market fountain overflowed in two silver rivulets. One of the company said, I never in all my life knew that this town was so pleasant. It seems to me that there is nowhere in the world a town as pleasant as ours.

That, responded his companion, is just what occurred to me this very moment.

Every city, remarked Rabbi Alter the slaughterer, in which decent and pleasant people live is decent and pleasant.

And now, added Rabbi Alter the teacher, those decent and pleasant people are going to go up to a truly pleasant place.

At that very moment one of the women was saying to another, I don't know what has come over me: for first I think that I have never seen such a lovely night, and then it seems to me, on the contrary, I have already seen such a night, and the very things I hear now I have heard before. I know that is not so, yet I cannot be certain it is not so.

To which her companion replied, Perhaps we have already journeyed once before to the Land of Israel, and everything we have heard and seen here we heard and saw before on some other night.

In that case, said the first, why are we here and not in the Land of Israel?

Comrade mine, said the other, we have already been there.

If we have already been there, said the first, how is it we are here?

Comrade mine, said the other, ere you go asking how we come to be here, I shall ask you how we came to be exiled from the Land of Israel and how we came to be scattered among the nations.

I cannot make out what you are talking about, said the first.

Comrade mine, said the other, didn't you tell me that it suddenly seemed to you that you had seen such a very night as this before?

Well, they hired themselves two long, high wagons covered with a kind of booth, and turned their household goods into money except for those utensils which they would require for the way; and they packed away their money in their clothes. They filled their boxes with pots and pans, and glasses and ladles and plates, and smoked meat, and fine pellets of baked dough that last a long time without going bad; and then they went to request permission from the dead to depart.

Some went to the graves of their fathers and their kindred, while others went to the graves of great pious folk, the constant props of the world, who had accepted burial outside the Land, entailing the pangs of having at the Last Judgment to make their way to the Land of Israel by rolling through caves and tunnels, all in order that meanwhile they might protect the town from evil decrees. At the graves our company burst out weeping, for they were very moved; the graves of the pious always arouse people to repentance. And they went on weeping until they reached the threshold of the House of the Living. There they turned their faces back to the graves and looked at them.

Then came Rabbi Abraham the circumciser, who had inducted more than half the town into the covenant of our Father Abraham, may he rest in peace. He took a circumcision knife and passed it under the soles of each and everyone of the company, saying, Children, I make this blade to cut under you in order that the dust of your city may not hold you. And he likewise passed the knife under his own feet.

Thereupon they all burst out weeping and went back home. They put on big boots especially prepared for the journey, with heavy iron nails on the soles to make them last a long time; the boots could be heard from one end of the town to the other when they walked. And that is why people in Buczacz say of noisy folk, They make as much noise in town as if they were going up to the Land of Israel.

They made the rounds of all the synagogues and Houses of Study in the town and passed through all the streets, discoursing about the Torah, praying and giving charity, so that they might never have to return to those places to make amends for any blemishes which they had been the cause of. Then they went from house to house to take leave of the living; and they asked each and every person separately, Perhaps you have something against me, or perhaps I owe you some money? Then they opened the collection boxes of Rabbi Meir of the Miracle and made bundles of the money to take it

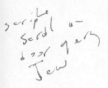

to their brethren in the Land of Israel; and they kissed each and every mezuzah on each and every doorpost, until they reached the river Stripa.

When they reached the Stripa, they paused to beg indulgence of the waters, saying, All the rivers run into the sea. We pray you, waters of the Stripa, do not be angry with us on our way. Finally they entered their own House of Study and prayed. At length they mounted their wagons, the men in one wagon and the women in another. The wagoner took the men's wagon and entrusted that of the women to Hananiah, whom he had appointed his assistant, as is the practice of wagoners who have two wagons and entrust one to one of the travelers and do not charge him any fare.

All the town went out to speed them on their journey, except the rabbi. For the rabbi used to say, Those who proceed to the Land of Israel before the coming of the Messiah remind me of the boys who run ahead of the bridegroom and bride on the way to the bridal canopy.

iii
The
departure

THEY departed the town and entrusted themselves to the horses. The horses lowered their heads and sniffed the way they were required to take. The wagoner mounted one wagon and Hananiah the other. Then the wagoner tugged at the horses' reins and urged them on. The horses raised their heads and prepared for the way, but still delayed their going, lest anyone had forgotten something and had to return. But nothing was to be heard save the sound of people weeping at leave-taking; so the horses lifted their legs and started off.

Hananiah took the whip in his right hand and cracked it over the heads of the horses, who turned their heads, looked at him, and went on. Those of the women who were accustomed to travel to markets and fairs said, Never in our lives have we had such an easy journey as this.

Are you a wagoner? the women then asked Hananiah.

No, said he, I am not a wagoner, but horses are horses and know what is required of them, so they go.

Are you telling me, said the wagoner to Hananiah, that you are not a wagoner? The very way you crack your whip shows that you are one.

Never did I drive a wagon and horses in my life, said Hananiah, except for the time when I saw a Jew and his horses drowning in the river and got them out and took him back to his home.

In this way they journeyed for nearly two hours through fields and forests and villages until they reached the Holy Congregation of Yaslovitz. Here the wagoner whistled to his horses and stopped the wagon, for it had been agreed in advance that the wayfarers would make a pause there in order to see their kinsfolk in the town before their departure.

There is no town so close to Buczacz as Yaslovitz. The head of one lies, as you might say, alongside the tail of the other; nevertheless, there is no peace and good will between them. Why? Because, when the old rabbi of Buczacz died, the town elders set their eyes on his brother-in-law who was rabbi in Yaslovitz, and desired to appoint him their head. They went and proposed the post to him, but he was not prepared to accept it.

Could it be, said he, that I should leave Yaslovitz, which is a small town where nobody disturbs me in my study, and go to a large town full of sages and merchants who give the rabbi no rest, the first with their casuistics, the second with their business?

Well, what did the Buczacz folk do but take a carriage and horses, and go into his house one night and seat him on the carriage and run off with him to Buczacz. It had barely grown light, when the whole of Buczacz shone with his honor and glory, while the light of Yaslovitz grew dim. Thereafter, whenever anyone from Buczacz went to Yaslovitz, the folk of Yaslovitz would quarrel with him and try to pull his hat off since Buczacz had taken away their crown.

Now however, since our company had left Buczacz behind them and were about to proceed to the Land of Israel, all the hatred of the Yaslovitz folk vanished; the whole town gathered together to honor them and received them with brandy and cakes and confectionery and fresh water which they brought from the well.

Even the Gentiles showed them respect on account of the honor in which the Land of Israel is held. Never was so much honor and respect shown in those parts. People actually prostrated themselves before the wayfarers, and kissed their garments, and gave fodder to their horses, on account of their affection for the Land of Israel; with the exception of the Armenians, who did not share in all this, since they are descended from Amalek and Amalek is the foe of Israel. The Armenians dwell all over the country and do business with the Orientals in peppers and spices and scents, thus competing with Israel; and their country is near the river Sambation, beyond which lie the lands of the Ten Tribes of Israel; and they wage war with the pious King Daniel who slays a thousand of them together, and who dwells in Armenia in the community called The Blood of the Chick; and he is a great and mighty king, tall as a giant, and thirty-one kings pay homage to him.

It is the custom among the Armenians, if one of them should smite and kill another, for the murderer to pay three hundred and sixty-five gold dinars corresponding to the three hundred and sixty-five veins and sinews of the human body; but they cannot do anything to Israel, because they were overcome long ago by Joshua.

After the men of good heart had refreshed themselves from the journey, they entered the Great Synagogue, which was the one that school children had found hidden in the hill and had cleaned out. There the Baal Shem Tov of blessed memory used to hide in an attic to study Kabbalah; and there his soul had been exalted unto heaven. Prayers said in the Great Synagogue are never in danger of idolatry, but all of them reach the Gates of Mercy entire.

There the men of good heart prayed that they might go up to the Land in peace and not be harmed on the way by packs of beasts or brigands, neither by land nor by sea. Then they went back and climbed into their wagons, and all the townsfolk accompanied them as far as the limits of a Sabbath day's journey. If you did not see the way the Yaslovitz folk gripped the hands of the Buczacz folk, you never have seen what affection is like in Israel. While the grown-ups stood shaking hands and embracing one another, the children patted the horses' tails, since their hands could not reach up to those of the folk in the wagons. And that is why they say in Yaslovitz when a little fellow tries to pretend to be grown-up, Go and stroke the horses.

iv
Temptation
on the
road

THE company traveled for several hours until they reached the Holy Congregation of Yagolnitzi, where they spent the night. In the morning they started out and came near Lashkovitz, that Lashkovitz where there is a great fair whose like is not to be found in the whole world; for more than a hundred thousand merchants come there year after year to do business with one another. At that particular time the fair was taking place, and they met small groups of merchants and wagons laden with all kinds of goods, so that the very earth groaned beneath them.

There it was that Satan came along and stood in their way and asked them, Where are you traveling?

To the Land of Israel, they answered him.

And how are you going to make your living over there? said he.

Some of us, said they, have sold houses, and others have other resources.

Don't you know, said Satan, that journeys eat up money?

We know it well, they answered. So each one of us has

labored to lay up money for the expenses of travel, for inns and the ship's fare.

And how about stuffing the pockets of the frontier guards? he asked. And who is going to pay poll tax for you to the King of the Ishmaelites?

How much does he ask? said they to him.

May you have the good luck, he answered, to have him leave you food enough for a single meal. Well then, what you must do is go to Lashkovitz and earn money. Happy is the man who dwells in the Land of Israel and does not need to be supported by the Holy Cities. How people toil to reach Lashkovitz! And now that you have come this far, will you go away without doing business?

Busy as he was with the men, Satan certainly did not ignore the women. Kerchiefs and headcloths and dresses he showed them, until their hearts were near bursting after the fashion of women who see fine clothes and covet them.

When your mother Rebecca, said Satan to the womenfolk, reached the Land of Israel, what did she do, according to the Holy Writ? Why, she took her veil and decked herself to show her loveliness in her fine things. And now you propose to go to the matriarchs and yet you don't behave as they did! Why, is Lashkovitz so far away? Why, it's in front of your noses. If a man sneezes here, people will say good health to him in Lashkovitz. Even the horses are turning towards it. The very beasts know where the road leads.

But Rabbi Shelomo took out his pouch and filled his pipe with cut tobacco leaf, and struck iron against a flint, and lit the pipe, and half closed his eyes, and began puffing out smoke fast, like a man who wants to get rid of a thought. He saw that the horses were gadding about in an unusual way, wanting to go on in one direction but actually going in another. Whereupon he touched the wagoner with the long stem of his pipe and said, Take yourself towards Borsztszow. And he urged him to hurry, since folks who proceed to the Land of Israel are like they who go to synagogue, and are duty-bound to run.

The wagoner cracked his whip, and tugged the reins one way and the other, and whistled to the horses, and turned them towards Borsztszow. The horses tossed their heads and dashed on until the dust rose from under their feet. At once the wagons with the goods in them vanished, and the whole countryside filled up with the lame, the halt, the blind, and every other kind of cripple carrying waxen models of limbs, models of hands and legs. For it is their custom to take these to the graves of the holy, there to set them up as candles in order that the holy men might see their deformities and remedy them.

Thereupon the men of good heart understood that all those enticements had come their way only to delay them, so that while they engaged in business to make money with which to live comfortably in the Land of Israel, their souls would depart from them outside the Land.

Like the king who invited his friends to a feast. The wise ones came at once, saying, Does the king lack anything in his palace? But the foolish friends delayed until they had filled their bellies with their own food so as not to require the food of the king. The result was that the wise friends were seated with the king and ate and drank of his best food and wished him well, while the others stayed at home and became drunk on their own wine and besmirched their garments, so that they could not even show themselves in the presence of the king. The king rejoiced at his wise friends and held them dearer than all the others, and was angry at the fools and introduced confusion in their midst.

In just the same way the King over all kings, the Holy One, blessed be he, invites those who love him to ascend to the Land of Israel. Is there anything lacking in the house of the King? say the wise ones, and proceed there at once and bless his great Name by the study of the Torah, with songs and praise; and the Holy One, blessed be he, rejoices to see them and does them honor. But the fools tarry at home until they fill their pockets with money, in order, as one might suppose, not to require anything of Him, blessed be he, in the Land of Israel. And at the last they grow drunk with their wine, that is, with money, and besmirch their garments, that is, the body, when buried in earth outside the Land.

Rabbi Alter the teacher spoke first and said, I hate the inclination to evil, which brings people to sin.

Rabbi Moshe responded in turn, The inclination to evil deserves to be hated, but I do not hate it; for all the merits I may have, come to me from the inclination to evil. But it is only just that the wicked should hate it, since it always leads them into evil; in spite of which, not only do they not hate it but they pursue it as though it were their own true love.

Well said, said Rabbi Shelomo.

But the wagoner said, Here are these people journeying to the Land of Israel and wanting to live on good terms with their evil inclination. I should not wonder if they take it along with them up to the Land of Israel.

Don't worry about us, said Leibush the butcher to him. Instead, just touch up your horses with the whip a bit, so that Satan will not overtake you on the road.

The wagoner turned his face to him angrily and said, And could I touch them up more if I had two whips?

Rabbi Yehuda Mendel looked with friendly eyes at Leibush the butcher, whose words amused him, and put his hands into his sleeves; for the day was already declining and the heat of the sun had diminished.

The wagoner took the reins and urged his horses on. They dashed ahead till they reached the village near Borsztszow where all wayfarers make a halt. The horses betook themselves towards the inn and pulled up at the stable door. The wagoner got down and unharnessed them, gave them their oats and watered them, while Hananiah aided our men of good heart and took down the pillows and cushions and all their other goods.

Then the travelers stretched their limbs and entered the inn to give rest to their bodies and to say the Afternoon and Evening Prayers.

v
*Welfare
and
wayfarers*

WHEN the innkeeper saw them, he stared in astonishment. Here they were, coming along to his place at the very time when the whole world, as you might say, was off to the fair. He put it to Rabbi Shelomo, who answered, That's how it is, you

Date **8/11** 19 **81**

Name

Address **ANN NORTON**

Sold by		Account Forward		
	NIGHTHEART			
	O/T SETS		4	95
				38
			5	33
	8			

IF ERROR IS FOUND RETURN THIS SLIP

THANK YOU
Call Again

———

**We appreciate your patronage
and hope we may continue to
merit it. If we please you, tell
your friends. If we don't, tell us.
We strive to satisfy.**

Stock 9-A Salesbook

see. The whole world goes *faring* downward, but we are *faring* upward.

To which Rabbi Alter the teacher added, You see, all the world is going to the fair, but we are leaving the fair aside and going up to the Land of Israel.

Well, the innkeeper was happy enough to have them since that was the case; and he went and fetched two bottles of brandy that they might wash away the dust of the road.

Which do you prefer? he asked them. The strong or the sweet?

Whereupon Rabbi Moshe clapped his hands with delight and cried, Oh, I love both the strong and the sweet.

The innkeeper supposed that Rabbi Moshe was talking about the liquor, but he was really referring to his Father in Heaven. And they said their blessings, and drank to long life, and said the Afternoon and Evening Prayers, the men inside the house and the womenfolk in the outer room.

Now several days had gone by in that house without a word of prayer being heard, and suddenly there was a whole quorum. The innkeeper and his wife had already been thinking of packing up and moving to the town where you can hear and take part in congregational prayer every day and all day long if you want to; but once a zaddik had stayed with them.

And how do you know, he had said to them, that the Holy One, blessed be he, requires your congregational prayers? Maybe what he wants of you is a glass of brandy and a dish of buckwheat groats. I assure you, this fine meal you serve wayfarers is as sweet to Him, as

34

you might say, as any of the fine hymns of praise they chant to Him in the town. So, on account of the words of that zaddik, they did not remove but did their best to serve wayfarers with food and drink.

While the company were standing and praying, the innkeeper's wife stood over her pots and pans preparing the evening meal. Happy the woman whose good fortune it is to have such guests come her way! Why, the very fire in the grate recognized the worth of the guests. Scarce had they finished their prayers when they found their supper ready, buckwheat groats boiled in milk which had come from the cow just before the Afternoon Prayer.

The company sat at the table, the men separate from the women. Rabbi Shmuel Yosef, the son of Rabbi Shalom Mordekhai ha-Levi, sweetened the meal with tales and legends recounting the praises of the Land of Israel. Desolate the Land might be, yet she remained as holy as ever, and Elijah, may he be remembered to good effect, still offers daily sacrifice in the Temple. Desolate though it be, the Temple is as holy as ever it was. The Patriarchs everlastingly stand at Elijah's side as witnesses and Heman and Asaph and Jeduthun are the choir. And from the skins of the offerings Elijah makes many a scroll on which he inscribes the many merits of Israel.

Well, having eaten and drunk and said grace, the men took books out of their sacks and sat down to study, while the women took out needles and wool and sat down to knit. The wagoner sent his horses to graze in the meadow but hobbled their legs that they might not stray off to the forest and be eaten by wild beasts.

35

Hananiah prepared the straw in the wagons and under the seats that there might be no delay when the time came for them to start out. Then he sat down in his own wagon and took out the Book of Psalms from his bundle and read by the light of the moon.

Gentiles from the village came to the door of the inn and took off their hats out of respect for the guests, saying, When there are guests in the house, God is in the house. The men of good heart sat silent, staring at these lofty countryfolk, who were tall as giants and whose hair was black as pitch and grew thick at the back of their necks, while it was cut short and shone over their foreheads. For they have no combs, and they grease their hair with lard and that is why it shines. And their beards are shaved and they clip their mustaches on either side; and their eyes are dark and gloomy with the servitude imposed upon them by their masters.

The chief of the villagers came over to the table and said, Spit into our eyes, O ye wayfarers to Palestine. At that Milka took out one of the honey cakes she had brought with her for the journey and shared it out among them. They lifted up their pieces to the level of their eyes and said, God's gift, God's gift. And then each man kissed his piece and put it in his bosom next to his heart. After that they took their leave and went.

Meanwhile Rabbi Alter the slaughterer saw Rabbi Leibush the butcher sitting in amazement. What are you amazed at? he asked.

Those Gentiles, answered Rabbi Leibush, have neither share nor inheritance in the Land of Israel and still they hold the Land of Israel so dear!

The reason, answered Rabbi Alter, is because of the

head of Esau which lies buried in the Cave of Machpelah.

Then the one whose name we have forgotten asked
Rabbi Yehudah Mendel, who is always known as the
pious Rabbi Yehudah Mendel, Why did Esau merit
having his head buried in the Cave of Machpelah?

The reason, replied the pious Rabbi Yehudah Mendel, is because Hushim, the son of Dan, took a stick and
hit Esau over the head so that his head fell off and fell
on the feet of Jacob; and they buried it with him.

That of course, said Rabbi Alter the teacher, is the
plain meaning; but there is a great and mystic secret
behind it as well. For during all the years that Jacob
was outside the Land of Israel, Esau was in the Land of
Israel, and its merits stood him in good stead. Indeed,
Jacob had already begun to fear that Esau and his sons
might gain the right to the Land of Israel; but then the
Holy Writ came and informed him that Israel are 'a
nation one in the Land,' and not Esau and his sons.
Then of course, you might argue that Ishmael had a
claim; but Writ has provided even for that in the verse
saying, 'The son of this bondwoman shall not be heir
with my son, even with Isaac.' Said the Holy One,
blessed be he: The Land is dear to me and so is Israel,
therefore I am going to bring Israel who is dear to me
into the Land which is dear to me.

Rabbi Shelomo brought out his long pipe and filled
the bowl with tobacco, and twisted himself a spool of
paper, and lit it, and began smoking, and looked in
friendly fashion at the company sitting and discussing
the Torah. How they had toiled before they left their
town; and how thoroughly weary and tired they are yet

37

to be. He raised his eyes aloft and meditated in his heart: We cannot know what to beseech of Thee; but as Thou hast done with us until now, so mayest Thou continue to do unto us forever.

The innkeeper's wife sat quietly gazing in front of her. There was a lighted candle on the table and the voice of Torah was heard continually in the whole house. Here in this inn which had been parched for words of Torah, those same words could now be heard rising on high.

While she was sitting there, a moth came and fell into the flame. How long had it lived? A moment. Just a few moments earlier it had been flying through the house, then for a little while it had gone circling round the flame, and at the last the flame had just licked it and turned it into so much cinder.

So it was with her. For a little while the Omnipresent had given her ample room; for a little while He had lit a great light for her; for a little while she had sat in this contentment, listening to the words of the living God; the next morning the guests would go their way and she would be left again without Torah, without prayer, and without life.

But while she was communing with herself, a number of countrywomen came in and curtsied to the pilgrims; they took a pile of pine cones from their aprons to place under the pillows of the wayfarers to Palestine, that they might sleep sweetly.

But the men of good heart were in no haste to sleep. Instead they sat studying and meditating on the Torah, while the women sat knitting socks and stockings for the journey. Sarah turned her head towards her husband Rabbi Moshe, as he sat with his head resting on his arm, holding a book in his hand. Her mind turned back to her two daughters whom she had left behind in Buczacz; now, she thought to herself, their husbands are just coming to eat their suppers, and maybe they too have boiled buckwheat in milk and are shaking fine sugar over the porridge to sweeten the food; but the men do not even notice the women's labor, but sit down at table and look into a book; sons-in-law like father-in-law.

While she was communing with herself, the woman next to her jogged her and said, Just take a look at Tzirel gazing at her husband Pesah as if they were all alone in the world. And Sarah, sighing, said, She who leaves nothing behind can be happy even when she leaves her town forever.

Well, the folk of good heart sat as long as they wished, until the wagoner came and advised them, You had better rest your limbs before the combs of the cocks turn white and you have to get up.

Sleep is fine for wayfarers, especially on Iyar nights in a village, when the whole world is still and the grass and the trees are silent and the beasts graze in the meadow and have no complaints against human beings. A gentle breeze is blowing outside and winding around the roof and rolling in the flower-cups of the straw which rustle, whispering with the breeze, making a man's sleep pleasant and sweetening his limbs.

But the men of good heart remembered that sleep was created only in order to strengthen the body that a man may rise fit and well for His blessed service. Before the third watch was over, they had all risen. At the same

39

time the Holy One, blessed be he, brought up the morning star; and the other stars and the planets began to
fade.

The clouds grew red and sailed away hither and
thither. The grasses and greenery began to drip and the
trees glistened with dew. The sun was about to appear,
and the birds clapped their wings and opened their
eyes to utter song. The horses whinnied and stamped
their hoofs and lifted their tails. The men of good heart
rose, and prayed, and ate the morning meal, and
climbed up on their wagons, the men on one wagon and
the women on the other. And they took their leave of
the inn and set out on their way.

vi
Through
the land
of Poland
and
Moldavia

THE wagons went on and on, the horses vanishing
and then reappearing in all manner of grasses,
tall and short. Pleasant breezes blew, rousing the spirit.
The grasses began to move to and fro in the fields and
made their utterances before the Holy One, blessed be
he. Many a village peeped out from the midst of the
fields, and vineyards and forests and lakes stood silent.
The sun shone on the rivers and on the riverbanks; and
white clouds bore the folk of good heart company from
the heavens.

And so they journeyed across the land of Poland until
they crossed the border and reached a spot called Okup,
where they safely crossed the river Dniester and spent a
night. From Okup they made their way to Hutin, which
lies on the right bank of the Dniester, and where there

are several Jewish householders dwelling in the shadow of the powers that be and managing to bear up under the Exile. These were engaged in commerce and handicrafts with great honor. When there were riots, the nobles would conceal them in their own homes and no harm would befall them.

It was their tradition that they and their forefathers had been dwelling in that place since the days of the Second Temple; except of course for those Jews who had come from Poland. For when the Tartars made forays into the Kingdom of Poland, they would take away captives whom they transported to the Land of Ishmael, which is Turkey, to sell them; and the kings of Poland used to send Jews to redeem them. Those Jews saw that it was a good land and thinly inhabited and that commodities were far cheaper than in other lands, and that the Jews who dwelt there lived on good terms with their neighbors and had no reason to fear them and merely paid a small amount to the king; so they came and settled there. At the old fort of Hutin a coin had been found dating from the time of the Royal House of the Hasmoneans, on which were engraved the name of Jerusalem and the figures of a bunch of grapes, a myrtle bough, and a citron.

Furthermore, living there were many women who did not know what had befallen their husbands, but there was no authority to deliver them from their fate, and they could not marry again. The husbands of some of them had gone to do business in Europe or Turkey and had not come back; the husbands of others had been slain on the way and their burial place was unknown.

One of these 'secluded' women joined our comrades

42

to make the journey with them. This was her sad story: Formerly she had dwelt with her husband and had borne him sons and daughters, never hearing a harsh word from his lips. His business had been dealing in horses which he bought for the nobles, who all trusted him and gave him money on account. He had never broken faith, neither in those matters which lie between one man and another nor in those that lie between a man and his God. But once he set out to buy horses with a lot of money in his possession and he never came back. It was plain when he never came back that he must have been slain on the road. His disappearance created a great commotion among the rest of the Jews and they set out in search of his body, asking many wayfarers whether they had seen such and such a Jew named Zusha, the horse dealer. Nobody admitted to having seen him, but some had heard that robbers had attacked a Jew and there was little chance that he had escaped alive from their hands. What was more, the same was said by an old wise Gentile woman who was versed in the stars. There is no sense in the Jews being excited, said she. That man has already left the world. The same was said in slightly different words by a Gentile who trafficked in witchcraft. The way he put it was, The Jews are not smart. They are spending their money for a tiny heap of bones. More than that he did not say, it being the practice of wizards not to say what they do not know. But when they entreated him to take pity on the woman and her children and to interpret his words, he said, The Jews are not smart. They are looking aboveground for what has already been put underground.

Now there was an old judge who was present and he

said, If he is referring to that Jewish robber chief who was hanged in the Land of the Ukraine, I can promise that they will not find him any more.

Now why should they have suspected that robber of having been Zusha? Well, several years earlier some Jews of that town had come and said that they had seen Zusha standing at the crossroads as a highwayman.

Here your wife and children, said they to him, are moving heaven and earth for your sake, and you . . .

Before ever they finished, other robbers arrived. But Zusha said, They are my townsmen. So they let them be.

Well, the Government heard about it and sent to capture him, but he was not to be found because he had already moved on to another country. Before long there came news that a robber chief had been caught in the Ukraine and there hanged; and the good name of the Jews was desecrated among the nations, because he was found to have a pair of phylacteries and thus identified as a Jew. And that was the last news to have been heard about Zusha.

But his wife took her children and went from one zaddik to another, weeping in their presence; but they had nothing to answer her. At last she came to the renowned Rabbi Meir of Primishlan, who told her, If you wish to weep, go to the place where the sea and the Danube weep for each other, and weep there. Meir has no love of tears. So she and her children were proceeding to the spot where the river Danube empties into the sea in order to seek her husband there.

The women sat knitting, tears falling from their eyes for this poor woman left 'secluded,' and for her husband who had died a sinner and left his children or-

44

phans. Yet the woman did not despair of her husband and was still searching for him; for, she argued to herself, could Zusha, who had lived at peace with every man and had always done his business so honestly, have joined a band of robbers and highwaymen? She was sure it was all a false charge.

The wagoner stopped his wagon and called to Hananiah, who came up level with him and stopped. Hananiah, said the wagoner, did you hear the story of the poor woman?

I heard it, Hananiah answered.

What do you think, Hananiah? went on the wagoner. Who is the robber they hanged?

It's my opinion as well, said Hananiah, that the fellow can have been nobody but Zusha.

The sun sank, sank again, and then sank once more. The women dropped their knitting needles, and wiped the tears from their eyes. Hananiah took out his kerchief and knotted it for a sign. In silence they rolled along the riverbank until they arrived at Lipkani, where they halted. From Lipkani they made their way towards Radiaitz, where the wagoner took off the horses' bells so that robbers and highwaymen might not hear them jingling. From there they made their way to Shtepenasht, a small town on the Basha river not far from the river Pruth.

From Shtepenasht they made their way to Jassy, where they arrived at dusk on the Sabbath eve. There are twenty-one large synagogues in Jassy, apart from one hundred and twenty Houses of Study and klauses and prayer rooms; yet when they came to Jassy, they did not pray in a single one of them but stayed at their inn

45

and constituted a prayer quorum for themselves, as the Sabbath had begun ere they had time to change their clothes.

But next day they hastened to the Great Synagogue, dressed in their Sabbath clothing and wearing their prayer shawls. By the time they reached the synagogue the congregation was already deep in prayer, since the folk of Jassy start early and leave early. Anyone who has never seen Jassy at her ease never saw a contented city in his life. More than twenty thousand Jews lived there, eating, drinking, rejoicing, and enjoying life. Among them, indeed, were some for whom the eating of Haman's ears at Purim was more important than eating unleavened bread at Passover. The holy men of the age labored greatly to make them stand erect instead of wallowing in the dust.

In brief, our men of good heart arrived in the midst of the prayers at a time when no man greets another. They stood where they were and nobody paid any attention to them. But when the time came to read the Torah, the warden summoned them to the reading. What was more, the warden summoned each one of them by his own name and the name of his father—except for Hananiah, whom he did not summon. It is the general custom that when a man comes to a place where he is not known and the warden wishes to summon him to the Torah, the man is asked for his name and the name of his father and then summoned; but this fellow summoned them without first asking any questions. If he was not a prophet, he was an angel or more than an angel; since even an angel has to ask, as we find in the case of Jacob, whom the angel asked, 'What is thy name?'

After the prayer was ended, the warden arranged a fine blessing over the wine in their honor, and while they sat together he asked each one of them about his affairs. They were astonished, for he told them everything that went on in their homes and their town. Yet from the way he ate and drank there was no sign that he was on a high spiritual level.

But once the wine went in, his secret came out.

Don't you recognize me? he asked them.

We have not the honor, they answered.

Then he said, Do you remember Yoshke Cossack, who once sold himself to the king's army for a skullcap full of money?

We remember, they replied, that they used to feed him on all kinds of dainties. If he wanted raisins and currants, they gave them to him. If he asked for Hungarian wine, he received it. If he wanted a bed with pillows and cushions, they had one prepared for him. When they took him off to serve the king, he asked for his pay to be doubled and they doubled it; and then, after all that, he ran away and deserted.

Would you suppose, said he to them, that he ran away to the Garden of Eden?

His actions, they responded, were not such as to indicate that there would be any place prepared for him in the Garden of Eden.

Well, said he, if you want to see him, just lift up your eyes and take a look at me. So then they stared at him and sure enough they recognized him.

There was another great marvel which our men of good heart saw in Jassy. This was a man with hair growing from the palm of his hand. On one occasion when folk had been talking of the coming of the Messiah, he held out his hand and said, There is as much chance for the Messiah to come as there is for hair to grow on the palm of my hand. Before he even had a chance to drop his hand to his side, there the hair was. He always wore a bandage around that hand and would take it off only to prove that we must never despair of the Redemption. Of course, the wiseacres who know everything had already tried pulling out the hair, for, they said, he must have it fixed on with paste; but by the next day the hair would have grown again.

On the day after the Sabbath they left Jassy and arrived at Vaslavi, a town on the river Vasli, which joins the river Barlad. In that town there is a great market for honey and wax, from which five hundred householders make a comfortable living. They spent the night there and next morning proceeded to the Holy Congregation of Barlad, so called after the river running through its midst. In this town there are two graveyards, one new, and the other old, in which people are no longer buried. It stands in the middle of the town and in it are the graves of martyrs killed for the sanctification of the Name; graves that are black as soot and face the east. They spent one night there and in the morning made their way to Tikotsh, a large town containing between five and six prayer quorums. There they spent a night and went on next morning to Avitshi, whence they journeyed to a large town called Galatz on the river Danube, where you take ship for the Black Sea, which the ships must cross in order to reach Stambul.

All the time that our comrades were journeying through this country, the wagons followed one another

48

through villages surrounded by meadows and vineyards and cucumber fields; flocks of sheep were scattered over the whole countryside, grazing in the meadows and drinking from the water troughs next to the wells; and shepherds sat piping pleasant tunes to them, tunes that were sweet and sad and sounded like the tunes that are sung in the House of Prayer on the Day of Atonement. How do Gentiles who tend sheep merit such holy music? This was once explained by Rabbi Israel Baal Shem Tov of blessed memory, who said that this people *(gentile shepherd)* have suffered a great deal but never denied their God, and therefore they merit piping the very music that Israel, who are holy, sing on a holy day and in a holy place before the Holy One, blessed be he.

So the wagons went their way with the horses pacing ahead, neighing and with their tails raised; other horses which they could not see answered them from the meadows, at which they would twitch their ears and pause. *horses* Countless sheep went by, crowding and thrusting one against the other, with their wool all in curls; and a cloud of dust rose all around the sheep as they walked, while a little shepherd strode behind them with a whistle in his mouth, playing to himself. Tall hills rose above the ground, now to the east and now to the west. Water ran down from the hills and the hills themselves came together, as if they did not want to let the wagons pass. But the handiness and skill of the wagoner and of Hananiah, who drove their horses expertly, got them out of the narrow pass. They entered one town and left another, and wherever they arrived the men of good heart were received with great affection. Beds were made ready for them and tables were set with food and drink: with *mamaliga* floating in butter, and with sheep cheese, and with wine; and when they departed the town, the cantor would accompany them singing the Sabbath verse, 'Happy in their departure.'

When our comrades arrived at Galatz, the party broke up. All the travelers awaited a ship which would take them to the Black Sea, while the wagoner went around looking for other wayfarers. The comrades sat in their inn and wrote letters to their brethren in Buczacz. They had much to write and they wrote much. This is the proper place to mention the good quill pens of the men of Galatz, which do not scratch or pierce the paper and do not splutter and scatter ink while writing; for since their geese are fat, the quills are soft.

The wagoner went to the market and hired out one wagon to the merchants of Leshkovitz, where the fair was still going on, since it sometimes lasted for four weeks and sometimes longer. The other wagon he loaded with sheepskins to take with him to Buczacz, trusting to the Lord that he would do good business with them.

But on the way he began to think, and his thoughts were disturbing. He thought to himself, What kind of fool am I to be going back to Buczacz, when those folk are going up to the Land of Israel? Here I have to water my horses and feed them hay, and do today what I did yesterday, and so every other day, until my time comes, and they lay me away in the ground with my teeth up, and the worms eat me. But why should I slip into thoughts of this kind? Has mine been a case of being able to go up to the Land and not wanting to? Rabbi

50

Abraham the circumciser was certainly worthy of going up, but if the Name, be blessed, did not want him to go up, he did not.

The sun was about to set and its rays gradually faded. The hills were covered over, and the moon came up and lit the way. Everything was silent. All that could be heard was the sound of the wells of the murderers; for it is a custom of the people of those parts when they kill somebody to dig a well to atone for their sin, and put a creaky pump on top.

The horses twitched their tails and their hoofs began slipping. The wagoner looked around him and saw that they had left the right path. He tugged at the reins and cracked his whip, shouting, Where are you dragging me to, you beasts? I'll show you the way to behave.

The horses lowered their heads and went the way they were required to go. And the wagoner wound the reins around his wrist and went back to thinking, now of himself, and now of Hananiah. This Hananiah fellow bundles his prayer shawl and phylacteries in his kerchief, and winds rags around his legs, and goes off to the Land of Israel, while all I do is go back to Buczacz. And why do I go back to Buczacz instead of going up to the Land of Israel? Because I am not prepared for the way. And when the Angel of Death comes, is he going to ask me whether I am ready?

While the wagoner was speaking to himself, his head sank on his chest. The horses turned their heads and saw that he was asleep. So they went ahead on their own accord, till suddenly they stopped. Whereupon the wagoner started up and took his whip and beat them until their flanks began to steam with sweat. And he yelled, Oh, you beasts, you always have to be sent off in a different direction from the way you want to go. By your lives, I shall thrash you until you forget that you are horses.

vii
Many
waters

WHEN the company arrived at Galatz they paid the tax required by the king of Ishmael, the Sultan of Turkey, and entered the town. There they found a market place full of food and drink, with all manner of delicacies and fruits whose names will not be found even in the chapter on blessings to be said over fruit in the volume, 'The Way of Life.' They bought provisions for the way, bread and wine and fruits and other things which sustain the heart. As for the people of Galatz, they showed their affection by giving them all kinds of conserves, to restore them while on the sea. Then the comrades shaved their heads and went to the bathhouse. The warm water drew the weariness out of their bodies, so that they really felt like new beings. After coming out, they hired themselves a ship and set sail on the river Danube until they reached a certain spot called Wilkup, where the river falls into the Black Sea and whence the ships go off to Constantinople. There they waited several days for the rage of the sea to die down, so that they might embark on a big ship.

When they arrived at Wilkup, it was already twilight. They set up a camp, said the Afternoon and Evening Prayers, and then repeated Psalm Sixty-nine which begins, 'Save me, O God, for the waters are come in even

52

unto the soul,' and which finishes joyfully, 'For God will save Zion . . . and they that love His name shall dwell therein.'

The sea was silent and the waters were still. The men took out the cushions and pillows and the pots and pans, while the women gathered wood, kindled a fire, and cooked the supper. Every day during their stay at that place Hananiah used to go out with the women and gather branches which dripped resin. These give off a fine smell when they burn and add a spice to the meal.

They sat on their boxes and ate their meal in the moonlight. The trees and plants smelled sweetly and the night too gave off many goodly odors; the water moved to and fro in the sea, the stars and planets gave light on high, and the earth whispered to itself below, restoring their souls. The good folk got up, spread out a place to sleep on the ground, and prepared to sleep, reciting the 'Hear O Israel' and praying for protection against demons, and evil and harmful spirits, and evil sins, and evil dreams, reminding His Blessed Name that they were dust and ashes and worms and corruption, and beseeching Him to forgive all their transgressions, as it is written, 'for with thee there is forgiveness.'

Suddenly they were pounced upon by every kind of mosquitoes, big as frogs, which bit them so that their faces swelled up. Never had they spent nights as bad as these. They could not sit, they could not lie, and they could not read any books. They could not sit up because of the mosquitoes, they could not lie down because of their sores, and they could not read any books because the mosquitoes covered the light.

This is the proper place to mention Rabbi Shmuel

Yosef, the son of Rabbi Shalom Mordekhai ha-Levi, who sweetened their sufferings with tales of the Land of the Sons of Moses and the Four Tribes who dwell beyond the river Sambation in large houses made of precious stones and pearls, and who need no lamps or candles at night, since the stones of their houses shine sevenfold brighter than any candle; furthermore, they live for a hundred and twenty years, and no son dies during the lifetime of his father, nor daughter during the lifetime of her mother. They are forty times as many as the numbers of those who left Egypt and possess all the good things of the world as a reward for their study of His blessed Torah and observance of His Commandments. There is nothing impure in all their borders, neither an impure domestic beast nor an impure beast of prey, nor impure birds, nor vermin, nor reptiles, nor flies, nor mosquitoes. And every day they hear a Divine Voice proclaim, 'Woe is me for I have destroyed my house, and burnt my mansion, and sent my children into exile.' And they wait for the Omnipresent to return them to the Land of Israel.

Great are the works of his Name, be blessed. Happy the man who devotes his heart to them and knows how to explain them to others. Happy is Rabbi Shmuel Yosef, who at all times can relate the good deeds which the Holy One, blessed be he, does for Israel. Every night that they were upon the sea Rabbi Shmuel Yosef cheered them with his words and told them tales of salvation and comfort; such as the tale of Rabbi Gad of Jerusalem, and the tale of Malkiel the Hero, and the tale of the letters which the Sons of Moses sent to the men of Jerusalem.

54

When day broke and the sea could be seen, the women began crying, Oh, we are afraid to set out on the sea, we are afraid to sail by ship; when a man dies on board ship they don't bury him but they tie him to a plank of wood and let him down into the sea! And then all kinds of big fish come, and some of them eat the soles of his feet while some eat his nose and lips. Last of all a big fish comes and swallows the corpse together with the plank which he is tied to, or else the sea spews him out on the sand, and all kinds of unclean birds come and peck out his eyes and pull the flesh off his bones. Whatever happens, the poor fellow never gets to a Jewish grave!

It was at that time that the women all made up their minds to go back to Buczacz, and screamed and cried for divorces. So they went off to the town and asked where a rabbi was to be found. But the folk of the town could not make out what they were talking about, for in those parts they do not have a rabbi, but a *hakham* who spends his time in the Yeshivah teaching the congregation Torah and right conduct. So the women asked, Then where is the judge?

We don't go in much for quarreling, said the people of the town, and so we do not need anyone to judge us.

But at last they found an ordained rabbi from the lands of His Imperial Majesty, the Kaiser of Austria, who happened to live in that town; and he arranged the divorces for the womenfolk. Then of course, after they had been divorced, the women remembered how folk buried outside the Holy Land must suffer by having to roll their corpses through caves and tunnels underground to reach the Holy Land. And they began

55

wailing aloud at the top of their voices. Each and everyone of them flung herself at the feet of the man who had been her husband and wept before him and entreated him, until the husbands arranged to take them under the bridal canopy and marry them all over again.

Then Rabbi Moshe said to Rabbi Yosef Meir, What a happy fellow you are, Rabbi Yosef Meir, to have given your wife her divorce before you started out, so that you no longer have to worry about divorces and marriages. Now here you have a Jew who wishes to prepare himself on the way in order to enter the Land of Israel with a clear mind. Suddenly his wife turns on him in a fury, wanting a divorce or demanding a bridal canopy. It is not good for a man to be alone; and when his wife is with him it is no good either. God forbid that I should complain about my virtuous paragon; but if you wish to study or if you wish to think some pure thoughts, up she comes with her talk and you have to devote your heart to what is a waste of time.

But Rabbi Yosef Meir only sighed and said nothing. He had never thought anything wrong with his wife, until the business of journeying to the Land of Israel came up, and then he had divorced her because she did not wish to go along; and once he had divorced her he had put her out of his mind. But now when the women were so disturbed at the sight of the sea, his divorced wife appeared before his mind's eye. Rabbi Yosef Meir said, Tomorrow the Holy One, blessed be his Name, will send us a good wind and I shall set off to the Land of Israel, while she, poor thing, remains forsaken outside the Land.

Within a few days the sea became calm and peace was

restored upon the waters. The waves that had thought to rise up and flood the whole world now flattened out when they reached the sand, and went back. The captain ordered the men and goods to come aboard. Thereupon each of the comrades took his goods in hand and went aboard, with his wife holding on to his tails and going up with him. Once they were on board, the sailors took oars in hand to make their way through the sea and began shouting, Hoya! Hoya! Within a very short while the wind began blowing on the masts and sails of the ships, and the ship began to move.

THE ship reached the point at sea where the waters move, and sailed along calmly. Our comrades stood reciting the Prayer of the Sea and the eight verses which Jonah had recited in the belly of the fish. Then, weeping, they sang Psalm One hundred and seven, which considers the kindness of the Lord and his wonders by land and sea, how he shall redeem his redeemed ones, and gather them together from all the lands, and lead them on the straight way, and satisfy the souls of those who hunger and thirst, and fill them with all good things; even if they reach the very gates of death, God forbid, He saves them by his mercies, and delivers them from their distress, and brings them to their desired haven; so that at the last they relate his deeds in song. Even if he raises the sea against them and brings up a stormy wind, he quiets the sea at once and silences the waves; and then they rejoice and give thanks to the

57

Holy One, blessed be he, and rise from their affliction, having seen that all that comes from the Lord is loving-kindness, but that it is necessary to consider wisely in order to see and rejoice in the mercies of the Lord.

After they finished reciting the entire Psalm, they sat down on their belongings, and took their books in hand, and read verses from the Pentateuch, the Prophets, and the Writings. When a man forsakes his home and reaches another place and finds a vessel which he had used at home, how he rejoices! How much pleasure he derives from the vessel! This is far truer of books, which are read and studied and engaged in every day. Thus Rabbi Moshe sits reading: 'The Land must be exceedingly good if the Lord desires us and brings us unto it and gives it unto us, a land which is flowing with milk and honey.' And Rabbi Yosef Meir sits reading, 'I have forsaken my house, I have cast off my heritage'; and both of them finished by reading together: 'Afterwards the Children of Israel will return and entreat the Lord their God and David their king, and they will fear the Lord and hope for His goodness.' Finally, they put the books down and rose, and each one placed his hand on the other's shoulder, and they sang:

> 'Oh that the salvation of Israel were come out of Zion!
> When the Lord turneth the captivity of his people,
> Let Jacob rejoice, let Israel be glad.'

The ship made her way quietly and a pleasant smell came up out of the sea. The waters moved after their fashion and the waves dwelt together in peace; while birds of some kind flew above the ship and beat their wings and shrieked. The sun sank below the horizon, the face of the sea turned black, and the Holy One, blessed be he, brought forth the moon and stars and set them to give light in the heavens.

One of the company looked out and saw a kind of light shining on the sea. Brother, said he to one of the comrades, perhaps you know what that is? But he did not know, and so he asked another of the company and that one asked still another.

Then they all turned their eyes and gazed at the sea and said, If that be the lower fire which comes from hell, then where is the smoke? And if it be the eye socket of Leviathan, then no eye has ever seen it.

Suppose, said Rabbi Alter the teacher, that it is one of the evil husks of the sea.

But Rabbi Shelomo said, It is time to say the Evening Prayer. Then they promptly rose and prepared to pray, since there is no evil husk or demon that has any power or authority over a full prayer quorum.

When they stood up to pray they saw that they were lacking one for a quorum. Hananiah, who had made the journey with them, had vanished. In the morning he had gone down to the market to buy his food, but he had never come back.

Then they began to beat their heads and to wail: Woe and alas, is that the way to treat a companion! It would have been better if we had gone back and been lost. We should have held one another's hands and come up into the ship all together, but we did not. When we came aboard, each one carried his own baggage and said, 'All is well, my soul!'

How hard Hananiah had toiled until he reached them! He had gone halfway round the world, and had been stripped naked, and had fallen among thieves, and

59

had forgotten when Sabbaths and festivals occurred,
and had profaned the Day of Atonement, and had made
his way barefoot, without boots. And then when he had
reached them he had gone to all kinds of trouble for
their sakes. He had rebound the books, and made cups
for the oil lamps and boxes for their goods, and had not
asked for any payment. All the trouble with the horses
had been left to him on the way; they had been happy
to have him because he would complete the prayer
quorum. But now that they had embarked on the ship
and were on the way to the Land of Israel, he had been
left behind. So they stood miserable and unhappy, la-
menting at heart because an unobtrusive vessel had
been in their midst and had been taken away from them
for their sins.

So everyone prayed separately, and while praying
they beat their heads against the sides of the ship in
order to divert their thoughts. Finally, everyone returned to his own place and sat down as though he were
in mourning. Gradually the night grew darker and the
ship went its accustomed way. The sailors tightened the
masts and sails and sat down to eat and drink, while
facing them our comrades sat, distress eating at their
hearts. Who knew where Hananiah could be? Maybe he
had been taken captive, God forbid, and sold as a slave.

The darkness grew thicker and thicker. Rats and
mice were scurrying around in the lower parts of the
ship and were gnawing at utensils and foodstuffs.

Where there is great anxiety, sleep helps to put it
right. But who could enjoy sleep when one of their
number had left them, and they had no way of knowing
whether he was alive or dead. How much Hananiah

had wandered about! How much trouble he had gone through! He had put himself in danger and disregarded his own life and had had no fear for his body, desiring only to go up to the Land of Israel; and yet now that his time had come to go up, something had gone wrong and he had not come aboard!

At the midnight hour the comrades sat on their baggage and uttered songs and prayers in honor of the great Name of Him who dwells in Zion. The stars moved in the sky, while the moon was now covered, now uncovered. The ship went on, the waters moved as usual, and a still small voice rose from the ship. It was the sound of song and praise rising from one firmament to another, till they reached the Gateway of White Sapphire where the prayers of Israel gather and join together until such time as the dawn comes to the Land of Israel. Corresponding to the prayers of Israel, praises of the Holy One, blessed be he, rise up from the waters.

Is it possible for water which has neither utterance nor speech so to praise the Holy One, blessed be he? But these sounds are the voices of the boys and girls who once flung themselves into the sea. After the wicked Titus destroyed Jerusalem, he brought three thousand ships and filled them with boys and girls. When they were out to sea, they said to one another, Was it not enough for us to have angered the Holy One, blessed be he, in his house, and now are we to be required to anger him in the land of Edom? Thereupon they all leaped into the sea together. What did the Holy One, blessed be he, do? He took them in his right hand and brought them to a great island planted with all manner of fine trees, and surrounded them with all kinds of beautifully col-

61

ored waves, blue and marble and alabaster, looking
like the stones of the Temple; and the plants from
which the Temple incense was made grow there. And
all those who saw that plant would weep and laugh.
They would weep because they remembered the glory
of the House, and they would laugh because the Holy
One, blessed be he, is destined to bring that glory back.

And the boys and girls still remain as innocent as
ever, fenced about from all iniquity, their faces like the
rosebud, just as we learn in the tale about the rose garden which was once to be found in Jerusalem. And the
brightness of their faces gives light like the planet
Venus, whose light comes from the shining of the Beasts
that are before God's throne.

And the children have no wrinkles either on their
brows or their faces, apart from two wrinkles under the
eyes from which their tears run down into the Great Sea
and cool the Gehenna of those sinners of Israel who
never lost their faith in the Land of Israel. These children are not subject to any prince or ruler, neither to
the king of Edom nor to the king of Ishmael, nor to any
flesh-and-blood monarch; but they stand in the shadow
of the Holy One, blessed be he, and call him Father and
he calls them my children. And all their lives long they
speak of the glory of Jerusalem and the glory of the
House, and the glory of the High Priests and the altar,
and of those who offered the sacrifices and those who
prepared the incense and those who made the shew-
bread.

And whenever the Holy One, blessed be he, remem-
bers his sons who have been exiled among the nations,
who have neither Temple nor altar of atonement, nor

High Priests nor Levites at their stations, nor kings and princes, he at once is filled with pity and takes those boys and girls in his arm and holds them to his heart and says to them, Sons and daughters mine, do you remember the glory of Jerusalem and the glory of Israel when the Temple still stood and Israel still possessed its splendor?

They at once begin telling Him what they saw in their childhood, and go on interpreting like Daniel, the beloved man, and Jonathan ben Uziel. The only difference is that Daniel and Jonathan wrote in Aramaic, while these children speak the Holy Tongue, which is the tongue the Holy One, blessed be he, uses. And at such times the Holy One, blessed be he, laughs with them; and you might say that at no other times does he laugh and smile as he does when he hears the praises of his House and the praises of those who came to his House. At such times he says, 'This is the people which I formed for Myself that they might tell of My praise.' And he also says, 'Comfort ye,' for in the future Jerusalem will be builded a thousand thousand times more great than she was, and the Temple will reach from one end of the world to the other and be as lofty as the stars of the heavens and the wheels of my divine Chariot; and the Divine Presence will rest upon each and every one of Israel; and each and every one of them will speak in the Holy Spirit.

Furthermore, all the years that those boys and girls have dwelt in the midst of the sea they have constantly awaited salvation, and there is no ship sailing to the Land of Israel which these boys and girls do not follow. For when they see a ship at sea, one says to the other, The

63

time has come for the Gathering of the Exiles. Thereupon, each of them takes one of the great sea waves and mounts it as a rider mounts his horse and rides until he comes near the ship.

And as they ride they sing, 'I will bring them back from Bashan, I will bring them back from the depths of the sea.' And their voices are as golden bells in the skirts of a garment, and they are heard by those who go down to the sea. Indeed we have heard a tale from such as tell only the truth, of how they were sailing to the Land of Israel on the Great Sea and heard a voice so sweet they wished to leap into the sea and follow that voice; but the sailors tied them up with their belts until the ship had sailed a distance away from the voice.

The moon sank, the stars went in, and the planets went their way. The Holy One, blessed be he, brought forth the dawn and lit up the world. As the dawn grew bright the travelers saw the likeness of a man on the sea. They stared and saw that he had a full beard, earlocks on either cheek and a book in his hand; and a kerchief was spread out under him and on it he sat as a man who sits at his ease. No wave of the sea rose to drown him, nor did any sea beast swallow him.

And what did the Gentiles say when they saw a man sitting on his kerchief and floating in the sea? Some of them said, Such things are often seen by seafarers and desert-farers. Others said, Whoever he is, he has a curse hanging over him so that nevermore can he rest. That is why he wanders from place to place, appearing yesterday on the dry land and today on the sea.

On that ship there were representatives of each of the seventy nations of the world, and each of them was overwhelmed and terrified at this apparition. So Israel stood on one side and the nations of the world on the other, fearful and staring, until their eyelashes became scorched by the sun. Then Rabbi Shmuel Yosef, the son of Rabbi Shalom Mordekhai ha-Levi, said, It is the Divine Presence, which is bringing back the people of Israel to their own place.

Vision seen as a sign

And Rabbi Moshe wept and said, 'The counsel of the Lord is with them that fear Him, and his covenant to make them know it.'

THE ship went on after her fashion and a pleasant odor rose from the water. Clear clouds floated in the sky and the waves kissed. The air was damp and had a salty tang. The fish thrust out their lips and amused the people, and the birds which fly about hither and thither not recognizing the authority of any man, nor associating with human beings, nor being fed by them, flew through the air and fluttered close to that shape out at sea. The waves went on rolling and the ship moved gently, not disturbing those in it overmuch. Our comrades sat, some of them conversing about the new souls that Israel, who are holy, receive in the Holy Land, while others were engaged in the secret questions of the universe, such as why the Land of Israel was first given to Canaan when it was actually intended for Israel. The reason being, of course, to instruct coming generations that although the nations rule over the Land of Israel and Israel is given into their hands, into the hands of

65

Sennacherib and Nebuchadnezzar and the wicked Titus, the nations are not resident there but are driven out, nation after nation, unsuccessful there and achieving nothing but destruction until they are expelled; but Israel are established in the Land for ever. Similarly, we find that the Holy One, blessed be he, gave Bathsheba to Uriah, the Hittite, although she had been intended for David ever since the six days of Creation. Uriah died without children, but an entire dynasty of kings and princes came from David.

poetic

The sun began to give way and returned to its place in order to make room for the moon and the stars. Stars and planets came and took up their posts in the sky, and the light shone back at them from the waves, and a sweet sound rose from the sea like the sound of song and praise.

One of the men said to another, Brother, do you hear that voice? What is it?

And the other said to him, The fish in the sea, brother mine, are uttering song. The same we find recorded in the special Section of Song in the Prayer Book, where it says, 'The fish in the sea utter song.' And the song they utter is, 'The voice of the Lord is upon the waters, the God of glory thundereth, even the Lord upon many waters.'

But his comrade said to him, No indeed, for I clearly heard a voice saying, 'My help cometh from the Lord, who made heaven and earth.'

That verse, answered the other, is uttered by the seagull; for that too we find in the Section of Song: 'The seagull says, "My help cometh from the Lord, who made heaven and earth."'

66

Let us also sing, said our comrades to one another. And thereupon one of them began singing:

'For a small moment have I forsaken thee,
But with great compassion will I gather thee.'

And his companions joined in the chorus, singing:

'And the ransomed of the Lord shall return,
And come with singing into Zion.'

The Holy One, blessed be he, has an excellent gift whose name is Sabbath, and because of his love and pity for Israel, he gave it to them. Great is the Sabbath, whose holiness shines even on ordinary people; for when the Sabbath comes, the Holy One, blessed be he, makes his blessed light to shine, and all created things shine with the higher illumination and yearn to cleave to his holiness. All the more is this true of pious hasidim and men of miraculous deeds, who reduce their own requirements and seek nothing but the pleasure and satisfaction of the Divine Presence.

When the morning before Sabbath eve arrived, our men of good heart rose early and began to prepare for the Sabbath. Rabbi Alter the slaughterer slew a fowl in honor of the Sabbath and burnt a garment and covered the blood with its ashes. Feiga kindled the fire and boiled the bird, while the other women engaged in cooking for the Sabbath. The captain passed them and looked at them with friendly eyes. Seeing this, the sailors brought them fish they had caught in the sea, and taught them to bake bread after the fashion of the Land of Beauty, the Holy Land, where coals are spread out on the ground and the dough is poured onto them. And so the women were able to fulfil the commandment of setting aside part of the Sabbath loaf, and they made

68

loaves for the feast of the Sabbath night and the feast of the Sabbath day and the third feast of the Speeding of the Sabbath; and ere noon everything was prepared for the Sabbath day.

Our men of good heart hastened to wash their faces and hands in hot water. They trimmed their nails, changed their clothes, and put on fine garments in honor of the Sabbath, an undergarment, an overgarment, a girdle, and a long coat. Then they sat down together and considered the deeds they had done during the six week days, and in their hearts considered the hidden purposes underlying the deeds of his Name, blessed be he, who had distinguished them for good from all the other folk in their town and given them the strength and courage to uproot themselves from their former home and to follow the right and clearly-marked way which goes up to the Land of Israel.

But their hearts bled and suffered for Hananiah, who had gone along with them all the time and had willingly taken upon himself all manner of suffering and anguish so long as he could go up to the Land of Israel; and then when he should have taken the boat, he had missed his opportunity and was left behind in the lands of the nations. Could the Holy One, blessed be he, still be angry with him for having forgotten when it was Sabbath and when the Day of Atonement? Was it his will not to admit Hananiah into his portion? Or was there some other purpose at work here, such as ordinary thought could not comprehend? At that moment a great awe took possession of their hearts, and they recognized that it had not been their righteousness which had allowed them to proceed to the Land of Israel but his blessed mercies. They were aroused to correct all the errors which they had made, in deed, in word, or in thought; in order that they should meet with no obstacle, God forbid, such as might delay the Higher Providence from bringing them to the Land of Israel. They also concentrated on elevating all the divisions of the soul and adding additional spirit to it. In this way the men of good heart sat together with their Maker until their ecstatic souls were awakened and an additional Sabbath soul was added to their own. They took their Pentateuchs and completed the study of the section of the week, reading it twice in the original Scripture and once in the Aramaic version, together with the explanations of Rashi; and they also recited the Song of Songs.

As for the women, they took out of their sacks the book of *Tehinnot,* which contains in Yiddish the prayers for the lighting of the Sabbath candles. They also brought out for study the volume called, 'Come Ye Forth and See,' which explains the Torah for women and ignorant people.

The sun descended into the sea to dip itself in honor of the Sabbath and stayed as long as was fitting. Sabbath is never ushered in on high until it has been ushered in below on earth. The women quickly removed the victuals from the coals, prepared the table with bread and wine, and lit the candles. The sun arrayed itself in a garb of many colors and entered the Mansion of Silence in order to usher in the Sabbath in the Assembly on High.

Our men of good heart stood and recited the Afternoon Prayer. The man who says the prayer beginning, 'Give thanks unto the Lord' with devotion assuredly feels the loving kindness of his Name, blessed be he, towards human beings; all the more so they that go down to the sea in ships, who see actually and with all their senses, the words and wonders of his Name, blessed be he.

They who recite the Eighteen Benedictions with devotion and say the prayer beginning, 'And mayest Thou return to Jerusalem Thy City in mercy,' assuredly draw near in spirit to Jerusalem. This is particularly true of those who sail on the sea; for when they pray, the Holy One, blessed be he, moves the boat and brings it closer to Jerusalem.

Since the six days of work were over and the profane week was at an end, our men of good heart stood singing the Psalm and song for the Sabbath day, until the whole world began to shine with the light of those crowns which had been taken from Israel because of the sin of the golden calf, and given to Moses, and which Moses returns to Israel every Sabbath eve.

After they had finished the Sabbath eve prayers, they hallowed the wine and bread, and broke bread, and ate and sang until the light of the candles came to an end and the light of the stars was doubled. When flesh and blood kindle a light it is doubtful whether it will take fire or not; and even if it does take fire it will go out. But the Holy One, blessed be he, kindles any number of lights in his heavens and not one of them goes out.

Great is the Sabbath, for then the body rests. Even greater is the Sabbath on board ship, when in any case a man does not toil all the week long and it follows that all the restfulness that is in a man can be kept solely and entirely for Sabbath.

Our men of good heart sat with their hands in their sleeves and looked out at the sea. When a man sits silent, it is assuredly a very good thing, since he is not sinning. This is particularly true when he is sitting in a ship that is going to the Land of Israel. Not only is he not sinning but he is actually fulfilling a commandment, since he is going up to the Land of Israel; and that is a deed which is accounted as equal to the fulfilment of all the other commandments.

All the commandments to be found in the Torah engage only part of the body. Thus the phylacteries occupy the head and the arm, and the fringes occupy the heart. Furthermore, they are fulfilled only during the daytime, and men are required to perform them while women are exempt. We are required to dwell in booths only at the Feast of Tabernacles, and again men are required to do this but women are exempt. Unleavened bread is enjoined upon us only at Passover, and the absolute requirement to eat it applies only to the first night. Furthermore, once a person is dead he is free from the fulfilment of the commandments. But dwelling in the Land of Israel encompasses a man's whole body and applies equally to men, women, and children, and it is required both by day and by night, and never under any conditions becomes null or void. Furthermore, if a person dies and is buried in the Land, its soil makes expiation for him, as it is written: 'And his Land doth make expiation for him.' Also this commandment is as weighty as all the others put together. So it is that when a Jew wishes to go up to the Land of Israel, Satan immediately gets in his way and does not permit him to do so.

Satans attempt
to keep
one
from to
going
Israel

Rabbi Alter the teacher began and said, When I was about to go up to the Land of Israel, Satan met me and asked, Where are you going?

To the Land of Israel, said I to him.

Why, he answered, I have just come back from half-way there because of the ants in the ship which got into all the food.

Indeed, said I to him, on the contrary, we can learn from them, as is written in the Book of Proverbs: 'Go to the ant, thou sluggard, consider her ways and be wise.' The ant, this little creature which is not one of those that have intelligence, still prepares its food in the summer. Then should not a man in Israel make prepa-rations?

Then Rabbi Moshe began, When I got on to the wagon to go to the Land of Israel, Satan was already there. Where are you going? said he to me.

To the Land of Israel, I answered.

It would be better for you, said he, if you were to stay in your place and serve your Creator with all the other decent householders, until the time comes for you to go up together with all Israel.

When I sold my house, I answered him, you were the one who whispered to me, Raise the price, go on, raise the price, because you are going up to the Holy Land! And now that I have sold my house, do you come and advise me not to go? I shall not listen to you.

Then Rabbi Shelomo began and said, When I set my mind on going up to the Land of Israel, Satan came along and said to me, Is an old man like you really pre-pared to go and lose the money he earned with so much toil and weariness?

74

Fine accounts you keep, I said to him. But then I also know how to balance the loss resulting from not keeping a commandment against the profit that comes from keeping it.

Then Rabbi Shmuel Yosef, the son of Rabbi Shalom Mordekhai ha-Levi took up the tale. When I was about to go to the Land of Israel, said he, Satan came to me and said, Where do you propose to go?

To the Land of Israel, I answered.

Why, said he to me, have you such a desire to go to the Land of Israel? Because so many of the commandments enjoined on Israel can only be fulfilled in the Land of Israel? By your life, there are still any number of commandments waiting for you to fulfil them outside the Land.

Wasn't it you, said I to him, who came to one of the zaddikim and advised him to fulfil all the commandments if only he did not fulfil one particular one? Surely you remember the answer you got from that zaddik. He told you, I am prepared to transgress against all the commandments, provided I fulfil this particular commandment in its entirety. And at that he let me be.

As for me, said Rabbi Yehudah Mendel the pious, Satan did not have to expend much effort on me, for he and I dwell together like two neighbors. When the idea occurred to me of going up to the Land of Israel, I said to myself, Why are people so afraid of going up to the Land of Israel? Because there is no food and drink? Because there are no human beings there like ourselves? Well, anybody who lives here can live there as well. After all, the Land of Israel was not given to the ministering angels; so why should I not go as well? Once

Satan heard this argument he stopped trying to delay me.

That, said Rabbi Pesah the warden, is exactly what I said to my wife Tzirel. What do you suppose, Tzirel, said I to her, that the Land of Israel is made of bits of paper on which holy names are inscribed? There as well as here you will find houses to live in, and there as well as here fat soups are not made from the juice of Hosannah willows.

In that case, said Leibush the butcher, why do they make the Land of Israel such a great affair?

Why, answered Rabbi Alter the slaughterer, in order that nothing wrong should be done in those same houses.

But Rabbi Yosef Meir sighed and said, It would be shameful indeed if all those houses were nothing more than what they seem to the eyes to be.

On still another occasion our men of good heart sat discussing the Evil Inclination which busies itself with Israel to prevent them from going up to the Land of Israel, since everyone who goes up to the Land of Israel there receives a new soul. Happy is he who goes up to the Land and has the merit of dwelling there, and alas for him who goes up to the Land and has not that merit; for angels surround the Land of Israel and permit none who are unfit to enter the Land, according to the tale told by Rabbi Shmuel Yosef, the son of Rabbi Shalom Mordekhai ha-Levi.

His tale concerns two old men who journeyed until they reached the frontier of the Land. At night they heard the sound of joy on the one side and of howling on the other. They raised their eyes and saw a troop of ministering angels, carrying harps and violins and all manner of musical instruments in their hands, leading one old man with great honor and singing before him; while in the other direction another troop of angels of wrath was dragging an old man and abusing him most shamefully.

By your charity, said the two old men to the angels, why did you make music before one and treat the other so shamefully?

He who is worthy to go up to the Land, said the ministering angels, him we accompany joyfully and precede with music.

But he, said the angels of wrath, who is not sufficiently worthy to go up to the Land but still goes up, him we drive away.

Perhaps, Rabbi Moshe asked Rabbi Shmuel Yosef, the son of Rabbi Shalom Mordekhai ha-Levi, you have heard why Rabbi Abraham the circumciser was never worthy to go up with us to the Land of Israel, seeing that he is a fit and proper man, God-fearing and greatly occupied with the fulfilments of the commandments and above all with the commandment of circumcision, in virtue of which we were given the Covenant of the Land?

Why, said Rabbi Shmuel Yosef, the son of Rabbi Shalom Mordekhai ha-Levi, the reason is that he put our Father Abraham to the trouble of leaving the Land of Israel and going forth outside the Land. For once there was a students' riot in town and all Israel hid themselves in their houses. Now on that very day Rabbi Abraham went to circumcise a baby whose father had just been slain on that same evil occasion. When he came in, he found nobody there to hold the baby, not even a chair on which to sit.

Can I, said he, be both godfather and circumciser?

Well, he looked out of the window and saw an old man walking along the street with a little stool in his hand. Rabbi Abraham knocked on the window to attract the old man's attention. In he came, sat down on the stool and took the baby on his knees. Then Rabbi Abraham circumcised the baby and said the blessing with the phrase, 'Who has hallowed the friend from the belly.' After Rabbi Abraham had completed the blessings, the unknown godfather vanished. Everyone thought that Elijah, the Angel of the Covenant, had been revealed to him, but in truth it was our Father Abraham who came to show his affection for his son on the day of his introduction into the covenant of Abraham.

All the countless heavens on high grew dark and the stars and moon were covered. The air was damp and had a salty tang. The whole world was still. Nothing was to be heard but the sound of the sea waves kissing. The company broke up and went to their sleeping places. The moon sank, the stars went in, and the planets went on their way.

The ship sailed on and on, while the Holy One, blessed be he, rolled the light away before the darkness and the darkness before the light, and sent a wind which moved the ship. Every day the sun grew stronger, so that no one could gaze at it, while at night each separate star gave as much light as the moon. And the sea waves swayed and moved and sparkled with light, and a ker-

chief floated upon the waves like a ship in the heart of
the sea; and a man sat on the kerchief, his face turned
to the east. Not a great wave of the sea rose to drown
him, no sea beast approached to swallow him, but the
seagulls soared and flew around him in the air. How
long the comrades had been on board ship you can
judge for yourselves; for before they went aboard they
had shaved their heads, and now the head phylactery
sank into the hair. Yet whenever they looked out to sea,
facing them they could see the light sparkling on the
waters, the kerchief floating like a ship in the heart of
the sea, and a man sitting upon the kerchief with his
face turned to the east.

IN due course the ship reached Kushta the Great,
which is Constantinople, which is Stambul. There
the comrades took a small boat and entered the town to
wait for the ship which is hired by the congregation of
Stambul every year; for every God-fearing Sephardic
Jew who has the means goes up to the Land of Israel to
prostrate himself upon the graves of the Fathers or to
settle there.

Now Stambul is a great city whose like is not to be
found anywhere in all the world, having many quarters
in which representatives of all the peoples dwell and the
king of Ishmael, the Great Turk, rules over them. Himself he lies on a bed of ivory which lulls him to sleep.
Sometimes he sleeps half a year and sometimes a whole

year. There is a box full of snuff beside him, with a gold bird resting upon it. When the time comes for the king to awaken, the bird opens the box and goes to the king and places the snuff in his nostrils; then the king sneezes and the bird says, Your good health!

Thereupon all the princes and pashas come along with all the dukes and ask the king how he is. And he has three hundred and sixty-five princes, one for each day of the year; and as soon as each of the princes has done his day's duty, the king gives him a golden thread, whereupon he knows that his time is come to depart from the world; he goes home and strangles himself, while the king, watching from his window, claps his hands and rejoices.

Then there is a clock in the king's palace, made of human bones, and on the hour it can be heard tolling from one end of the city to the other. Even babes still in their mother's wombs quiver at the sound. And the city has many gardens and orchards and bathhouses and places of amusement, each more beautiful than the next —beautiful within but filthy without. Numberless dogs roam the streets; nowhere in all the world are there so many dogs as in Stambul. And unclean birds stroll about at their ease, gorging on the filth and the carrion. There are also rats as large as geese; and these dwell even in the mansions of the princes.

Furthermore, there are many fires in Stambul, and when a fire begins in one house, the licking flames consume all the houses in the whole street, since their houses are made of wood. Sometimes these fires burn three hundred or four hundred houses together, and sometimes even more. They take no steps to stop the fire; only, the watchmen of the city stand shouting, Allah is God and Mohammed is his Prophet.

The synagogues in Stambul are many, numbering a hundred and more, with rugs and carpets woven of gold and silver thread, on which great sages recline and teach the revealed and the secret Torah. They have many books in their possession and happy is the eye that has seen them all. Why, they even have that rare and precious volume, 'Desire of the Days,' which is a wonder, as the well-informed know. They exercise their authority by permission of the state and do not understand our own Yiddish tongue. So when anyone wishes to talk to them, he must speak in the Holy Tongue. They are clean in thought, and cleanly in dress, and pleasant in speech, and all their deeds are done gently, and their figures are princely.

Their customs differ from our own, and they put on their phylacteries while seated, in accordance with the view of the book, 'The House of Joseph' by the sage Rabbi Joseph Karo. Some of them indeed put on two pairs of phylacteries at the same time. They have no fondness for casuistry when they study the Talmud, their great strength being rather in erudition. But the love of the Land of Israel burns in their hearts, and when they go up to the Land of Israel they take with them the carpets on which they have studied Torah and burn them on the grave of Rabbi Simeon bar Yohai on the thirty-third day of the Counting of the Omer.

There are Karaites to be found in Stambul who do not believe in the words of our rabbis of blessed memory but they are versed in Scripture and are as familiar with the twenty-four books of the Bible as an ordinary Jew is

with his prayers; and they have synagogues of their
own. They do not wear fringes as our own Jews do, but
hang them up in the synagogue and look upon them in
order to fulfil the injunction, 'that ye may look upon it';
and they do the same with the palm fronds at the Feast
of Booths. They have sages of their own who produce
fresh interpretations and commentaries on the Torah
every day; but they have no quarrel with our own Jews,
since they must have recourse to us. For inasmuch as
they still observe all the biblical laws of purity and pol-
lution and do not pollute themselves by attending to
the dead when any of their own community dies, they
must hire poor rabbinist Jews to perform the last offices
of burial. In former times they used to sit in the dark on
the Sabbath eve and kindled no light, until the light of
our teachers was revealed to them. The Land of Israel
is precious to them; they mourn over its destruction and
donate vessels and money to their own House of Study
in Jerusalem and find all kinds of excuses in order to go
up and increase their number in the Holy City.

But they are not successful, for they behaved shamefully towards the works of our master, Rabbi Moshe
ben Maimon of blessed memory. For it happened on
one occasion that the sages of Jerusalem had to take
counsel in secret on account of impending evil decrees
and events. So they gathered in the synagogue of the
Karaites, whose synagogue lies lower than the other
houses, so that no word said within it is heard outside.
When they entered they saw that one step in the stair-
case differed from all the others. They investigated and
found underneath that step a copy of Rabbi Moshe ben
Maimon's book, 'The Mighty Hand,' which had been

82

placed there by the Karaites to be trodden upon and belittled.

Now the Kabbalist Rabbi Hayyim ben Attar of Morocco, who is known as the 'Light of Life' after his book of that name, was present on that occasion and he cursed the Karaites, saying, May their settlement never increase and may they never be worthy to pray with a full quorum. Since then no new Karaite has ever arrived in Jerusalem without another Karaite being carried out dead. Once a great number of Karaites went up to the Land together and were all carried off by the pestilence, may the Merciful One deliver us.

Well, our comrades stayed in Stambul waiting for a ship. One day they went to the grave of Job, and another they went to the grave of the author of 'The Ordination of the Sages,' who died there on his way to the Land of Israel; and yet another day they went to the port to see if a ship had arrived bringing Hananiah, of whom they did not yet despair. Was it possible that this Hananiah who had wandered over half the world and had overcome so many trials could have given way to despair when his ship went off without him? Assuredly he must have possessed his soul in patience and waited for another ship.

During those days Rabbi Shmuel Yosef, the son of Rabbi Shalom Mordekhai ha-Levi, sat before the sages of Constantinople and read all those books, great and small, good and upright, which are full of the fear of Heaven and of wisdom; and he increased in reverence and wisdom of the revealed and secret Torah, in grammar and in style, in the ways of the holy language and its secrets. There has come unto our hands a letter

83

which he wrote to the society of the comrades, the hasidim who dwell in the city of Buczacz, may it increase. It runs thus:

We hereby inform you that we have reached in peace that glorious city Kushta, which is hinted at in the mystical work, 'The Additions to the Book of Splendor'; and blessed be his Name, for the way before us was good. Rain did not detain us on land nor storm terrify us on sea. Indeed it were fit and proper to indite all our journeyings and all the good deeds done unto us on the way by our brethren, the Children of Israel, in respect to food, drink, and lodging, and in respect to good counsel and proper guidance, by our brethren in the country of the Turk no less than those in the Land of His Imperial Majesty, the Emperor of Austria. However, by reason of our sorrow at heart, we are deprived of the strength to continue with this account at length, for the upright Rabbi Hananiah, who is known unto you, did vanish of a sudden on the way. We do not know what has happened to him; but pray you to give notice of this to the Gaon and the Head of the Court, long life to him. Indeed, we are aware that Rabbi Hananiah did not leave any wife behind him. Yet it may be there is a woman who is waiting for him to marry or reject her, according to the Law. Pray inform us how goes it with the learned, pious, etc., Rabbi Abraham the circumciser, may he increase in strength, and all that has befallen him; and pray transmit our regards to all our friends and those beloved of our soul who are forever engraved on our hearts; and so on and so forth.

In the inn where the comrades lodged there was a

certain Sephardic sage, who had gone forth from the Holy Land as an emissary to rouse the cities of the Exile to remember the distress of the men of Jerusalem. He was an understanding and scholarly man, a Kabbalist whose figure was kingly and whose eyes had grown dim on account of the tears he shed, mourning that every city stands firm on its foundations, but the city of God is abased to the nether Sheol. *netherworld*

This emissary asked our friends, Whither do you go and where do you wish to establish yourselves? In Jerusalem, or in Hebron, or in Safed, or in Tiberias? He told them the advantages and qualities of each of the cities and the virtues of its particular climate, also the holy places to be found in each. *guide to nearby holy cities*

As for Safed, he who dwells in Safed and is buried in its soil, since it is loftier and has pleasanter air than all the other cities of the Land of Israel, his soul soars off at once to the Cave of Machpelah, whence it passes to the Garden of Eden. In Safed, Israel are at peace with the Gentiles, so that even a woman can go about alone in the town and the field. There are many dwellings to be found in Safed, and everything can be bought cheaply. The synagogue of the Kabbalist Rabbi Isaac Luria is in Safed, together with the platform to which he used to summon the Fathers of the World, of blessed memory, to the reading of the Torah; summoning Aaron first as Priest, then Moses as Levite, Abraham as third reader, and so on. Most of the men of Safed are observant of the Torah, and scholarly, and God-fearing, and merciful. *Safed*

Two hours distant from Safed is a place called Meron, *Meron*

85

where the cave of Rabbi Simeon ben Yohai is to be found. From all the cities of the Land of Israel men come to Meron three times a year to prostrate themselves on his grave, where they spend a night and a day and study the holy 'Book of Splendor'; these three times being in Elul, before the New Year, at the end of the month of Adar between Purim and Passover, and on the thirty-third day of the Counting of the Omer after Passover. Furthermore, on the thirty-third day of the Omer people come to Meron even from as far away as Damascus and Aram Zoba, which is Aleppo, as well as from Egypt; and in Meron they set beautiful silken kerchiefs on fire in barrels of olive oil and they make great feasts and banquets and dance to the drum and the pipe and utter all manner of song and praise. That is the day of the Rejoicing of Rabbi Simeon bar Yohai, when the Divine Presence comes to frolic with the saintly in the Holy Assembly.

Even greater is Hebron, whose dust the Fathers esteemed. They lie in the Cave of Machpelah, above which is a great building builded by King David, peace be upon him; although by reason of our sins Israel are not permitted to enter the Cave. But there is a small hole outside the gate which opens on the graves of the Fathers and the Mothers, and there candles are lit and prayers are said. Outside the Cave of Machpelah is the nearby grave of Rabbi Moshe ben Nahman of blessed memory; as he wrote at the end of his book, 'The Law of Men,' where he said that he was going to hew himself a grave there near the Fathers. Facing it is the grave of Jesse, the father of David, as well as the grave of the

86

judge Othniel, the son of Kenaz. Below are caves where other pious men are buried.

The householders of Hebron are men of might with many fine qualities, above all hospitality, a virtue for which our Father Abraham, peace be upon him, was renowned. And the whole town is surrounded by vineyards and groves, and you can see the oaks of Mamre, and the bathing pool of our Mother Sarah, peace be upon her, and the tent of our Father Abraham, peace be upon him; the which tent is fenced about with blocks of hewn stone. There is a cistern of hewn stone within the tent, and fresh living water sweet as honey and very pleasant to drink flows within the cistern.

But how good it is to dwell in Tiberias, which is Rakkath—where even the most worthless are as full of fulfilled commandments as a pomegranate is of seeds, and where they are more nimble about their affairs than in any of the other cities of the Land of Israel. As our rabbis of blessed memory said: 'May it be my lot to be among those who welcome the Sabbath in Tiberias.'

T. Serius

Four kinds of plants are plenteous in Tiberias, particularly the date palms, whose fronds are used to cover the booths for the Feast of Booths. And the Sea of Kinnereth, which the Holy One, blessed be he, loves more than every other sea surrounds Tiberias; and concealed in that sea is the well of Miriam, which is destined to be revealed in due course by the holy Rabbi Isaac Luria of blessed memory; for it heals the soul. Corresponding to the well of Miriam, the baths of Tiberias make the body hale and hearty and cure all manner of sickness. And in the future the revival of the dead will commence at

Tiberias, where the redemption will likewise begin, as is written in the tractate Rosh ha-Shanah, Leaf Thirty-one.

Yet in spite of all this, who would exchange the sanctity of Jerusalem, the place of our Temple, for any of these? For Jerusalem faces towards the Gate of Heaven.

xi
A great
storm
at sea

IN due course the time came for the ship to set sail on the sea. The comrades went aboard together with a vast congregation of Sephardic Jews from Stambul, Smyrna, and all the other cities belonging to the Turk, both men and women; not to mention uncircumcised Christians and circumcised Moslems of all nationalities; more than a thousand folk in all, apart from the servants of the ships and the servants of the servants.

They put down their goods and prayed that they might arrive in peace in the Land of Israel, and that they might not be injured on the way by earthquakes or convulsions or by any of the creatures that are in the sea. When they had ended their prayer, they split into two parties. One party went to see where the sweet water was drawn from and where wood was got for cooking, while the other went off to look at the ship and watch the sailors at work, standing high upon the masts or rolling up the ropes or spreading the sails. Meanwhile, our Sephardic brethren settled in their places, and calmly opened their sacks, and arranged their belongings, and took out fine volumes bound in red and green leather, covered with papers of many colors, like the picture tapestries hanging in the king's palace. They sat down crossing their legs beneath them, and prayed that they might be worthy to walk before the Lord in the Land of Life and be buried in Jerusalem.

How pleasant it was to see them sitting in fine garments, with their measured movements and princely appearance, their beards resting on their books as they read in awe and fear and humility, their lips moving and their attention fixed, rejoicing in the study of those things that are befitting persons proceeding to the Land of Israel. Their wives sat facing them, holding in their mouths pipes which were fixed in round glass bottles through which they inhaled tobacco. Whenever they heard the name of Jerusalem uttered by their husbands, they would raise their hands to their eyes and joyously repeat the word aloud, kissing their fingertips as though the name of Jerusalem were there engraved.

Meanwhile, the sky threw the sun over its shoulder, and the water began to grow darker and darker. The *poetic* ship's officers examined the ropes and spars, lit lamps, sat down to eat and drink, and began to sing songs about wine and about the women of the sea who turn their eyes on human beings and steal their souls away with their singing. The Jews (mark the distinction) said the Evening Prayer and restored their souls with refreshments, reading the Song of Songs and the section in 'The Book of Splendor' concerning the Complete Unity which the Holy One, blessed be he, will achieve with the Congregation of Israel in days to come. Feiga and Tzirel, the housewives and stewardesses of the group, arranged pleasant sleeping places for themselves and their companions. They lay down to sleep and rested their bodies until they arose for the Midnight Mourning.

The stars gave light and then were hidden, but others came and took up their posts. Our men of good heart rose for the Midnight Mourning, while their Sephardic brethren ground peas and boiled *kahava*, a kind of drink which rouses the heart and causes sleep to depart, and which is not known in the Land of Poland, although it is mentioned in the 'Ordered Table.' They also behaved generously towards their Ashkenazic brethren, giving them likewise to drink; and they did the same with their wine and books. And when it became necessary, the Sephardic brethren spoke well of them to the ship's officers and men, the sages of the Sephardim being well versed in the languages of the peoples, some among them even knowing the seventy tongues, like the members of the Sanhedrin in days of old.

Three weeks passed peacefully. The ship's crew subdued the waters, the ship moved gently and our men of good heart sat studying Scripture and Talmud or else relating the praises of the Land of Israel. Rabbi Shmuel Yosef, the son of Rabbi Shalom Mordekhai ha-Levi, made the time pass sweetly with those praiseworthy legends wherein the Land of Israel is praised. As a king who spreads a curtain over the entrance to his palace for whoever is wise to roll back and enter, so did Rabbi Shmuel Yosef roll back the gates of Jerusalem before them and enter with them to discover all that lay innermost.

Facing them sat our Sephardic brethren, who are not versed in the Yiddish tongue of the men of Poland; but they saw the joy of their brethren and asked, Why are you so happy? and were answered in the Holy Tongue: Thus and thus did Rabbi Shmuel Yosef relate to us.

Then they also wanted to listen, and Rabbi Shmuel Yosef immediately opened his mouth and began to speak in the Holy Tongue like unto the ministering angels, relating the praises of Jerusalem and the joy with which the Divine Presence would rejoice in them. For ever since the day when the Temple was destroyed, there is no day without its vexation, the Holy One, blessed be he, having long sworn that he would not enter the Jerusalem on high until such time as Israel would enter the Jerusalem below. And our Sephardic brethren, listening, could have kissed him on the mouth for those words.

Three weeks passed peacefully. The ship sailed along quietly. The sun gave light by day and the moon by night. The sky was full of stars and the sea behaved after its fashion, while the waves went along as one who goes to a festivity. But on the bed of the sea the waters began grumbling, and the wind began slapping at the masts of the ship. At last a great storm arose and the ship rocked this way and that, sometimes to the right and sometimes to the left, sometimes sinking and sometimes rising and rearing up, the waves wrestling angrily with the ship, ready to swallow the ship and all who dwelt therein. The whole sea was covered with foam as though the Great Sea had been transformed into a Sea of Foam.

Happy is he who rests on such a night in the shadow of his own house, and the four walls of his house surround him and his roof protects him from the rain so that he can lie on his bed and cover himself with a warm blanket and listen to the sound of the footsteps of the night watchman passing in front of his house. Then in the morning he can put on his prayer shawl, and crown himself with phylacteries, and say his prayers in the House of Prayer, and calmly eat his meal, and go out to the market place, and engage in business honestly, spending his days and his years honorably and passing away with a good name, worthy of burial with his fathers.

But on that night the eyes of the comrades were deprived of sleep and their body of rest. All their bedding was soaked with salt water. There were sixty myriads of waves spitting in their faces and roaring. Where was the river Stripa where they used to dip themselves on Sabbath eve on sunny days, and where they would cast away their sins on the New Year's Day? Why, the river Stripa was hundreds of leagues away. Now they were in the midst of the sea, and waves as huge as mountains were rising to the sky, and the ship was being slung about like a stone from a sling. And the sailors were growing too weak to steer the rudder much longer and subdue the waters.

All those on board were thrown against the sides of the ship, and screamed and wept and wailed. A chill salt sweat appeared on their faces, drops of salt dripped from their hair and rolled down into their mouths. Some of the comrades brought up their mother's milk, while others felt their bellies near bursting. I do not wish you such a passage, all ye seafarers!

At midnight the storm grew worse, and breached the walls of the ship. The ropes began to part and the noise grew ever greater. No one could be heard above the sound of the waters. There arose a great tumult among the people on board the ship. One man raised his hands and cried for aid, while another tore his hair. There was no one to subdue the waters and no one to aid a comrade in the hour of his distress. Yet mention must be made of the captain, who remained at his post and encouraged the sailors not to despair of mercy and not to slacken their labor.

In a little while the ship started and shook more than ever, as though it had struck a reef and were about to break. All the gear was tossed high into the air, and falling struck the people down. When our men of good heart saw that they were indeed in danger, they said: When our holy rabbis of blessed memory went to the Land of Israel, namely, Rabbi Nahman of Horodanki and Rabbi Mendele of Primishlan and all the other pious men like them, they were in such distress as this on the sea. Then Rabbi Nahman took the Torah Scroll on his arm and said, Even if, God forbid, the Court on High has decreed that we must pass from this world, nevertheless, we, a court on earth, together with the Holy One, blessed be he, and his Divine Presence, do not concur in that decree. And all those present responded, Amen.

At that moment a sailor mounted to the masthead and said, Looking through my glass I espy the cities of the Land of Israel.

Those, said our men of good heart to themselves, were indeed great pious men, mighty heroes. May it be His will that we may be delivered from this distress, on account of their merits and the merits of the Land of Israel.

Their prayers achieved one half and the ship's men

93

achieved the other half, and the Holy One, blessed be he, in his blessed mercy achieved the whole. Within a few moments the fury of the Prince of the Sea died down, and the face of the waters changed for the better. That day passed without mishap, nor did any evil befall them at night. The moon came out and gave light, and the ship proceeded peacefully. The sick gradually regained their health.

Gradually the moon turned pale. It was already time for the sun to rise. In the twilight of dawn the waters of the sea grew silent and a kind of reddish veil spread over the face of the waters. The ship stood still in the midst of the sea, powerless to move, and a mood of relief passed through everyone.

Brethren, said one of our comrades, do you know what I say to you? I am like a person who is shown the king's treasure house. The attendants go down into the cellars with him and his feet stumble, but since he knows where they are taking him and that it is to the king's treasure house, he rejoices.

'Who shall ascend into the mountain of the Lord,' responded Rabbi Yosef Meir, 'and who shall stand in His holy place?'

When the sea burst forth, said Rabbi Shmuel Yosef, the son of Rabbi Shalom Mordekhai ha-Levi, and was about to flood the ship, what was I thinking of at that time but the story of the holy Rabbi Shmelke, may his merits shield us.

Once upon a time a very harsh decree was to be imposed on the men of the Holy Congregation of Nikolsburg, but the king had not yet set his seal to it. So the holy sage journeyed to Vienna to the king. It happened to be the season when the ice was melting, and at that time the river cannot be crossed by ship. Go, said Rabbi Shmelke to his holy disciple Rabbi Moshe Leib of Sasov, and fetch me a trough. He went and fetched a trough and put it in the river. They got into the trough and stood erect. The holy Gaon chanted the Song of the Red Sea and his holy disciple responded, until they reached Vienna safely. The folk of Vienna stood staring at two Jews crossing the river in a small trough at a time when it cannot be crossed even by a ship, because chunks of ice as large as hills float about in the river, crashing together with great fury and roaring like thunder.

The king heard what had happened. He came out together with his lords and princes and saw two Jews standing upright in a trough and chanting, while huge chunks of ice as big as hills were crashing together in the river, not touching the trough, but parting and making way for it to pass safely through. No sooner did that zaddik reach the king when the king said to him, I shall certainly listen to you, holy man of God, and he annulled the decree.

Well, said Rabbi Alter the teacher, what do you think of that story?

Oho, said Rabbi Alter the slaughterer, where shall we find such a trough today!

Feiga sighed and said, We are traveling in a big ship, not to a king of flesh and blood but to the King who is King over all kings, the Holy One, blessed be he, and we see no signs of betterment.

And Tzirel said, That is just what I was about to say: here we are on our way to the Land of Israel and not as much as the smell of a miracle.

95

But Milka silenced them, saying, Women, you are ungrateful, for is the Holy One, blessed be he, showing us so few signs and wonders? He put the understanding in our hearts to go to the Land of Israel, and led us peacefully and safely across the land and set us on a good way with no obstacles or mishaps, and provided us with a ship to set sail on the sea, and took a wind out of his treasury to set the ship going. Then when the sea began quaking round us, He silenced it and ordered the Prince of the Sea to control his anger, which he did, so that the water began moving gently again, and in a day's time he will be fetching us to the Land of Israel. And *you* say that He is not showing us any sign of His goodness! Lord of the Universe, what ought Hananiah to have said? How that Hananiah toiled! He went on foot from town to town and from country to country, and the frontier guards took away his money and stripped him naked, and he was taken captive by robbers, and forgot when the Sabbath occurs and profaned the Holy Day, and wandered about many days, all in order to go up to the Land of Israel! And then when the time came for him to embark, the ship set off and left him behind.

Yes, said Rabbi Alter the teacher, that's the way to talk, the way Milka talks. By your lives, while she was speaking every limb of mine could feel the miracles that have been done for us!

But once they came to talk about Hananiah, their faces twisted with grief on account of the poor fellow who had actually thrown away everything for the sake of the Land of Israel; and then when his time came to go aboard ship and proceed to the Land of Israel, the ship had gone off and left him behind, and nobody

96

knew whether, God forbid, he was dead. Yet in spite of the grief in their hearts, their eyes shone as the eyes of good people shine when they talk about a good man.

Then Rabbi Pesah the warden said, Do you remember Hananiah's kerchief in which he kept all his goods? When he would stand up to pray he would take out his things and tie the kerchief round his loins as a prayer girdle. On one occasion I said to him, Hananiah, here is a girdle for you so that you needn't shift your things about, in and out and out and in; but he wouldn't take it. And what answer do you think he gave me?

You have to treat a vessel respectfully, said he, and even if you find a better, you mustn't put your first vessel out of use. And he gave the same answer to Milka. On the way Milka gave him a sack for his belongings, but next day she found him with his bundle tied up in his kerchief again. Didn't I give you a sack for your belongings? said she to him.

You did, said he.

And still you go on using your kerchief, said she.

And do you think, he said, that just because a kerchief hasn't any mouth, I have the right to treat it dis-respectfully?

At that point Rabbi Alter the teacher interrupted and said, Now that the Omnipresent has made things easier and the sea has quieted down, it is proper for us to say the Morning Prayer.

But after they had prayed they could not eat anything because the sea water had spoiled their food. The Holy One, blessed be he, salted the Leviathan for the end of days when it will be eaten, and the sea has been left full of salt. But who needs food and drink when he is going

97

to reach the Land of Israel in a day's time? The comrades had already heard that the ship was approaching the port and promptly forgot all the toil of the journey and the difficulties of living on board ship and the storm at sea. Legs that had been heavy as stone suddenly became light, while eyes that had been sore with weeping now shone like the dawn.

They all put on their Sabbath garments and adorned themselves in honor of the Land, taking great care that none of the dust of Exile should be upon their clothing, that they might enter the Land pure.

Rabbi Moshe had a little bag suspended round his neck containing earth from the Land of Israel, to be buried with him. Now when they were expecting to enter the Land, he opened the sack and emptied the earth into the sea.

Our sages of blessed memory, remarked Rabbi Moshe, said that in days to come the Land of Israel will expand all over the world. For that reason I fling this earth from the Land of Israel into the sea, in order that an island may grow up from it whereon shall be built a great city of the Land of Israel.

Then they all began singing and uttering praise because it was their merit to be approaching the Land of Israel. And they arranged their belongings and tied them around with ropes, not to be delayed when the time came to go ashore.

But it was not yet their appointed time to stand in the Royal Palace. When the sailors climbed the masthead to see where they were, they gazed and saw the likeness of a large city; it was neither Jaffa nor Acre nor Tyre nor Sidon, nor any other of the coastal cities of the

Land of Israel, but the city of Stambul. Then the hands of 'them that handled the oar' grew weak and they were seized with trembling. Here they had spent three weeks and more trying to reach the shores of the Land of Israel and at the end the winds had taken hold of the ship and brought it back to Stambul! The Holy One, blessed be he, had perhaps wished to test his invited guests and to see whether they were fit to serve in his legion; so he had brought a stormwind upon them and taken them back to their starting place. Those who wished to go up to the Land of Israel could remain on board, while those who wished to return to the lands of Ishmael and Edom might so return. But they all responded as one, We shall go up at once! We shall not go back!

The captain sent the sailors to fetch food from the city, since all the food they had on board had gone bad; and the sailors took their oars and got into ramshackle boats and went to town and fetched back all the good things from the land of Ishmael. The ship spread its sails, the captain took up anchor and the Holy One, blessed be he, promptly drew out a wind from his treasury and broke its force, saying to it, Be careful not to injure my friends. And the ship started off and ran joyously ahead, as one who joins in a dance.

Lightning does not strike twice in the same place. Blessed be He who led them on the right way by sea and by land, and by sea again. The ship proceeded quietly for five days and nights and arrived safely near Jaffa. When the morning star rose on the sixth day, the last day of their journeying, Jaffa rose from the sea like the round sun floating up from the River of Fire to light up the world. That was Jaffa before them, Jaffa which is the gateway to the City of God, into which the exiles of Israel come in order to go up to Jerusalem.

The morning star rose higher and higher, the sun shone more and more brightly, and it began to be really hot on board ship. The fire from on high branched out and it became burning hot. The sailors took off most of their clothes, for they were sweating like bears. And the Jews (mark the difference!) likewise took off their upper garments, and removed the hats they wore over their skullcaps and fanned their faces with them; but they continued to simmer in their sweat and the sun, simmering the sweat again, dried their bodies to the very marrow of their bones.

While they were sitting fanning themselves, Leibush the butcher asked Rabbi Alter the slaughterer, Tell me, Rabbi Alter, what need is there for this sun?

Why, he answered, the Holy One, blessed be he, is roasting the Leviathan for the great feast of the righteous at the end of days, and that is why he has heated the sun to the boiling point.

What is happening to me? said one of the women to another. My eyes are growing dim!

Do you think, answered the other, that my eyes are made of glass? I feel as though they were being pierced with white-hot spits.

That's not the sun in the sky, said Tzirel, but a fiery oven.

But Rabbi Moshe overheard them and said, No, your eyes are growing dim because of the radiance of the Divine Presence.

Even Feiga, who had made the journey for love of the Land of Israel, could not feel satisfied with what she saw. Where were those pleasant breezes which, people said, blew all day long among pleasant gardens and groves of myrtles and palms and citrons? And all the mountains of spices and odors like those in the Garden of Eden? Here the fires of hell were descending and burning the very marrow of their bones. Had the ship lost its way and strayed, God forbid, into a desolate wilderness of fiery serpents and scorpions, and were all manner of fresh woes about to descend upon them? The womenfolk knew that the Land of Israel is in ruins and that many troubles dog a person's heels; but they preferred to remember what suited them and to forget what did not suit them.

Milka sat across the way, smiling.

Are you grinning at me? said Feiga to Milka.

It's not you I am grinning at, answered Milka, but myself. In my dreams I saw a long and beautiful mantle at Lashkowitz to wrap one's whole body in, and I wanted to buy it. And now do you know what I am thinking? If I had bought it, what could I have done with it? Why, wrap up the sun in it so that it should not catch a chill.

In my dreams, I too, answered Feiga, was sitting in a wagon and a fur coat appeared to me and I heard someone or other whisper, Just you go along to the fair at Lashkowitz, for there are all kinds of bargains waiting for you there.

And did you suppose that Satan had our good in mind? said Milka. All he wanted was to hold us up on the road.

The sun stood in the middle of the sky, heating up the ship, which became as hot as a pot resting on coals.

Yet he in whose heart the love of the Land of Israel is fixed gathers strength from the sanctity of the Land, where the Higher Light still flows freely and without any hindrance, though the Land is in ruins.

Meanwhile the men of good heart withdrew their attention from the toils and troubles of their wayfaring and from all the devils who had hindered them, and their faces were aflame with the force of their perfect will. Rabbi Alter the teacher stretched out his hands and began tapping the box before him with his fingers and singing the mystical hymn beginning, 'Sons of the Heavenly Hall, who yearn,' and Rabbi Alter the slaughterer accompanied him with, 'May they be with us . . .'

Ere the day was over, the ship reached the Jaffa shore and fired a loud cannon. Arabs came out of the town, wearing miserable clothing, short and dirty shirts reaching only to their knees and tied round with a thick rope, and the soles of their stockingless feet were covered only with slippers. They spoke noisily as though they were quarreling, and nobody could make head or tail of their language. Up they came on board, yelling at the top of their voices. They dragged the folk away like captives, and took their goods and flung them down into their ramshackle boats. They took their fee, yet even that was not enough for them, and they wanted to beat our comrades; but the Holy One, blessed be he, rescued them from the Arabs' hands and brought them safe and sound to shore.

AS soon as our men of good heart reached the shore they flung themselves on the ground, kissed the earth, and burst into loud weeping, until their eyes streamed like wells. How is it possible for children who return to their father's home and find it ruined not to weep? Yet even in their mourning they rejoiced because they had been worthy to return home. They took one another by the hand and sang, 'I rejoiced when they said unto me, Let us go up unto the house of the Lord.' Furthermore they sang, 'The Lord loveth the gates of Zion more than all the dwellings of Jacob.' And the Ishmaelites stood in the distance staring.

And so they went their way singing until they were brought to a certain courtyard known as the Courtyard of the Jews. There they found chambers, one for prayer with the congregation when they were ten together, and two more known as the Holy Chambers where there were beds for the use of the sick people coming from the journey; one chamber for men and the other for women. And there was another chamber there which was the chamber of the beasts, where the beasts on which people rode up to Jerusalem were stabled.

When a caravan that has been on a journey reaches its destination, the travelers assuredly rejoice, particularly if they have been in great distress and have come forth from it; for then indeed they have good reason to rejoice. But when one of the group is missing and nobody knows whether he is alive or dead, the thought of

him is bound to come up no matter how much they rejoice and to disturb their joy. So it was with our comrades. For Hananiah had gone through so much together with them and had passed through so many adventures on his own in order to go up to the Land of
Israel. And then when his time had come to go up to the
Land he had not done so, and they did not know
whether he was alive or dead; so how could their joy be
complete? They vowed to have his name commemo-
rated in Jerusalem and to pray for him at the Holy
Places.

And now it is fitting to find out what happened to
him—to Hananiah, that is. When his comrades went to
fetch victuals for the journey, he went along with them.
But on the way he parted from them and went in a different direction, but they did not notice it. After a while
he came back and did not find them. Off he went to the
port. When he came there, he saw that their ship had
already set sail. How the poor fellow had toiled and
labored in order to go up to the Land of Israel! And
now when his time had actually come, the ship had
started off and left him behind, and he stood watching
and could not go with it!

Now Hananiah was always quick and nimble; so
what had held him up on the way? Well, while he was
standing in the market, a Gentile came along.

Aren't you the fellow, said Hananiah to him, who
wished to lead me to the Land of Israel through some
cave or other?

Yes, said he, I am the man.

And what are you doing here? asked Hananiah.

I don't know any more than you, said the other. Every day when I put on the phylacteries of our former robber chief, I hear him weeping for his wife and children, and now I am wandering through the world in search of them.

May you live a hundred years, said Hananiah to him. You are earning your share of the world-to-come. Come along with me.

They went to a certain house, and Hananiah knocked on the window. The householder opened the window and asked, What do you want?

Where is the woman, answered Hananiah, who came here from Hutin?

I do not know, said the other. She went out with her children this morning and has not come back. Perhaps she has already gone off to Hutin.

On hearing this, Hananiah sighed and said nothing.

What do you need that woman for? asked the householder.

Hananiah pointed to the Gentile and said, This fellow can bear witness as to where he last saw her husband.

It would be a good thing, said the householder, if he were able to give his evidence before a rabbi.

While Hananiah was talking to the householder, the Gentile went to one side to put on his phylacteries. No sooner had he done so when the woman came along and shrieked, Oh, those are my husband's phylacteries!

If Zusha is your husband's name, said the Gentile, then these are his phylacteries; and he promptly handed them over to her and told her the whole story of Zusha. And that was what caused Hananiah to be delayed.

There are ever so many tales about salvation, each

finer than the next; like the story of the man who was lost in the desert. Suddenly a huge bird appeared and lifted him on its wings and in a single hour flew with him to his house, a distance it would have taken several years to journey. But no bird came to Hananiah. An even greater wonder was the mantle of King Solomon, peace be upon him, for he would sit on it and the wind would bear it away, so that King Solomon could eat his breakfast in Damascus and his supper in Media, though the one is in the East and the other is in the West. But that mantle has vanished since the day that King Solomon, peace be upon him, passed away, and nobody knows where it is concealed. And even if Hananiah were to find it, he would not be able to do anything with it, since nobody in the world ever knew how to sit upon it except Solomon and his four princes: one the prince of humanity, and one the prince of the demons, and one the prince of the beasts, and one the prince of the birds. Likewise, even in the generation before our own miracles were performed upon the water, such as that of the holy sage Rabbi Shmelke of Nikolsburg and his holy disciple Rabbi Moshe Leib of Sasov, who crossed the river Danube in a trough in a dangerous season. But where is such a trough to be found nowadays?

So Hananiah, seeing that he was indeed in distress, raised his eyes to the sky and said, Lord of the Universe, I have nothing on which to depend except on your many mercies.

Thereupon the Holy One, blessed be he, gave Hananiah the idea of spreading out his kerchief on the sea and sitting upon it. So he spread his kerchief upon the sea and sat down upon it. The kerchief promptly floated off to sea, carrying him upon it all the way to the Land of Israel. Nor was that all. For he actually got there before his comrades, who were first delayed at Stambul waiting for a ship, and then found themselves in distress during the storm at sea; whereas he crossed the sea peacefully.

Now let us return to all our other comrades. In brief, they reached the sea of Jaffa, that same sea of Jaffa which is kept in store for the pious in days to come. For at Jaffa the Great Sea brings up all the ships that are lost anywhere upon it, together with their gold, and silver, and jewels and pearls, and glassware, and valuable vessels, and in time to come the Messiah King will give each of the righteous his share of the wealth.

They got off the ship and into a ramshackle Arab boat. The sailors took their oars and shouted, Yoho and Oho, and subdued the waters and made passage through the sea, and led the boat between sharp rocks which have been there ever since the Creation. For before any of the waves in any of the seas and rivers start out on their journey, they come to prostrate themselves before the sea of the Land of Israel; and if the sharp edges of the sea did not break their force, never a ship would be able to reach Jaffa on account of all the waves.

They came safely forth from the sea and from its sharp teeth, and received all their goods intact, and came up on the shore at Jaffa, the threshold of the gate of the City of God. There they flung themselves on the ground, kissed the earth, wept over the ruin of the Land, and rejoiced that they had been worthy to arrive.

Then came two wardens and led them to the Court

of the Jews, which was a hostelry for the Exiles of Israel. This court was surrounded by a wall, and fine trees were planted in it, and it had its own well of water in the center of it. They stood and prayed according to the usage of their own land and restored their souls after the journey. There they stayed until they obtained animals for proceeding to Jerusalem. They went out knowing that all was good, on the day whereon God twice saw that his handiwork was good, namely the third day of the week; and they traveled until evening, when the air grew chill.

Then they got down from their asses, opened their sacks, took out their cushions and pillows and covered themselves; but still they felt cold. So they got back on their asses and went on until they reached a certain spot called Ramleh, which is the city of Gath that David captured from the Philistines. There they descended from their asses and made themselves a resting place, arranging their sacks and lying down there all night long until the morning star arose.

When the morning star arose, they said their prayers, and ate the morning meal, and mounted their asses and resumed their journey. At nightfall they reached a well. They got down from their asses, made themselves a resting place there, lay down to rest on their sacks, and slept until the morning star arose.

When the morning star arose, they said their prayers, and ate the morning meal, and then got on their asses and journeyed until they reached a certain spot called Motza, from which in ancient times willow boughs were brought to the altar, as we learn: 'There is a place below Jerusalem called Motza, to which people go down to gather willow boughs which they afterwards set up beside the altar.' And willows are still to be found there.

There they made a resting place and stopped over. All these ways are desolate because of robbers, and even the Ishmaelites themselves dare not pass on these ways unless they go out in a caravan together. But his Name, be blessed, took pity on our comrades, so that no mishap occurred to them on the road except that their sacks fell from the backs of the asses once or twice. There are chains of high and lofty mountains all along the way, with all manner of clouds covering them, clouds of blue and purple, clouds radiant and gently bright, with the radiance of the jewels and blossoms of the Garden of Eden.

Every hour a new light made its appearance, and none of the lights resembled one another; and goodly odors there were on every side, issuing from all manner of fragrant plants. And castles, and palaces whose beauty was once the glory of the country now stand desolate, and there is no settled place, nothing but the black tents of Kedar dispersed and forsaken among the mountains, and goats trailing down the mountainsides, sustaining themselves on the thorns and thistles and brambles and briars mentioned in the Scriptures; and half-naked men sit there, wearing nothing but a shirt and girdle and a black kerchief bound by a woolen rope on their heads. And fine springs and streams of water run down into the valleys from the mountains, and they taste like the springs in the Garden of Eden. Our comrades drank of those waters, and in those waters washed their hands before the prayer, and rinsed their eyes because of their tears over the destruction of the Land, and hallowed their hands in honor of the Holy City.

This they did for three days, until the Sabbath eve arrived, and the Holy City, the joy of the whole world, appeared before them in the distance. At once they descended from their asses and rent their garments, weeping bitterly, and proceeded on foot until they reached the gates of Jerusalem. They kissed the stones of her walls and rent their garments a second time in memory of the Temple. May it be His will that it shall be rebuilded speedily and in our own days. Amen.

WITHIN a very short while their arrival became known throughout the city. All Jerusalem came forth to meet them, both the pious and the devoted scholars; and they wished them peace, greatly rejoicing in them and offering them every manner of honor, and saying to them, Happy you are to have come hither without considering your bodies and your wealth, but thinking only of your souls; so that you have been found worthy to stand in the Temple of the King who is King over all kings, the Holy One, blessed be he.

And the rabbi of the hasidim, the chief of the Sephardic sages in the Holy City, showed his great love for the men of 'Turkey' and brought them to his own House of Study, where every day and every night they held soul-satisfying gatherings.

These they continued for four weeks corresponding to the four periods in a man's life: the first week being for the week of birth, when the infant grows and is not yet completed, for which reason he is not subject to punishment in the Assembly on High, until he has reached the age of twenty years; then a second week corresponding to his best years which last until he is forty, these being the choice years of a man's life when a man's strength is on the increase; the third week corresponding to middle age, when he gradually grows weaker; and a last week corresponding to old age, when a man runs the course of his days and years to their completion until he passes away.

But the dead of the Land of Israel are not thought of as dead, but are described as being stationed beneath the Seat of Glory, where they enjoy the light of the Messiah and see the happy state of Israel and all those fine things which the Holy One, blessed be he, will in time to come do for Israel. And on those occasions when the day grows dark, the dead do not become startled or cry out, for they know that the darkness is due to the clouds which go forth to carry Israel and bring them back to Jerusalem; as was expounded by our rabbis, who said that the time will come when Jerusalem will be like unto the Land of Israel and the Land of Israel will be like unto the whole wide world, and the clouds will carry Israel from the ends of the world and will bring them to Jerusalem; this being why the prophet praises them, saying, 'Who are these that fly as a cloud?' And every Sabbath they enter into the Assembly on High where they study the portion of the week as expounded by Adam, by Enoch, by Noah, by Shem and

Eber, by Melchizedek, by Abraham, Isaac, and Jacob, and by Moses, Aaron, and the seventy elders; in addition of course to the story of the Creation as far as the completion of Heaven and earth and the resting of God on the seventh day, and in addition to the whole of Jacob's blessing to his sons at the close of the Book of Genesis, which they learn from the very mouth of the Almighty. And at the Sabbath Afternoon Prayer, all the prophets come and teach them the section from the prophets, and Rabbi Abraham ibn Ezra, of blessed memory, interprets the difficult passages, since often when the prophets prophesied they themselves did not know what they were prophesying. Of all Rabbi Abraham ibn Ezra's interpretations the most highly thought of is the one of the verse beginning, 'And he [Jacob] bought the parcel of land,' which Rabbi Abraham ibn Ezra explains as indicating what a great virtue is in the Land of Israel, for a portion in the Land of Israel is reckoned as though it were a share in the world-to-come.

But now let us return to our comrades. In brief, they were welcomed by the Holy Congregation of Jerusalem with every manner of honor and respect, and the people of the city showed their affection by taking our comrades to their homes, and fetching them food and drink, and preparing them beds with pillows and cushions. They refreshed themselves and rested their weary bones until noon, when they went to the bath to purify themselves in honor of the Sabbath and in honor of the city. And the bath of Jerusalem is the most praiseworthy of baths, because it has inner and outer rooms. In the outer rooms people take off their clothes, in the inner they wash naked. And there is a room in which attendants rub down the bathers after they have finished their baths. And they have an oven there under the ground, which is stoked with animal droppings and manure. All the rooms are hot, some hot and some hotter; there are reservoirs of water and a perennial pool of fresh water, which is neither hot nor cold, but lukewarm. The bather pays two pennies to the bathing master and one to the attendant and receives a sheet for modesty's sake.

Well, they went down and dipped themselves in the ritual bath. Then they went up and sweated and afterwards proceeded to the room where the attendant rubbed them down and poured cold water over them. They went and dipped once again, came up and dried themselves, put on white garments, and came out like newborn creatures. And when they came out they gave the attendant a penny, and he wished them good health. Back they went to their homes, put on Sabbath garments, and proceeded to the Western Wall.

Now the Western Wall is all we have left of our beloved Temple since ancient times. It has been left by the Holy One, blessed be he, by reason of his great pity for us, and is twelve times as tall as a man, corresponding to the Twelve Tribes, in order that each man in Israel should devote his heart and will to prayer in accordance with his height and his tribe. It is built of great stones, each stone being five ells by six, and their like is not to be found in any building in the world; and they stand without pitch or mortar or lime between them, in spite of which they are as firmly united as if they were one stone, like the Assembly of Israel which has not even the slightest sovereign power to hold it together, yet is,

nonetheless, one unit throughout the world. Facing the
Wall on both sides are courtyards belonging to Arabs,
who dwell there with their beasts and do not disturb
Israel in their prayers.

Our men of good heart kneeled, and prostrated themselves, and kneeled, and took off their shoes, and washed
their hands, and walked with bowed head until they
reached the Wall, and weeping kissed each and every
stone. Then they opened their prayer books and recited
the Song of Songs with great passion and devotion, their
souls being aroused more and more with every verse.
Rabbi Moshe rested his head against the Wall and remembered that he was standing at a spot from which
the Divine Presence itself had never moved. He began
reciting the Song of Songs with awesome fervor and
with the very chant with which his brother, Rabbi Gershon, may he rest in peace, had recited it at the time his
soul departed from him, until he reached the verse beginning, 'The King hath brought me into his chambers,'
saying which Rabbi Gershon, his brother, had departed
from the world. But here Rabbi Moshe managed to
complete the entire verse, the joy of the Land of Israel
entered into him, together with a fresh vitality.

After they had completed the Song of Songs, they
recited a number of psalms and said the Afternoon
Prayer. And they added a special prayer for their brethren in exile, and for Hananiah who had vanished. Much
had they wept for him upon the sea and much had they
wept for him upon the dry land; yet all those tears together were but as a single drop in the sea against the
tears they shed for his sake before the Western Wall; for

they felt the sanctity of the Place, and he was not there with them.

This can be compared to a story about a king's friends who came to visit him and the king showed them his treasures. While they were standing before the king, they remembered that a certain person whom the king loved above all others had not come with them. So they began to grieve on his account, because he was not there to see what the king was showing them; they grieved all the more as he had been far more zealous on the journey than all of them, and the king would assuredly have been pleased and contented with him. Hananiah was worthy of standing at their head, and now at the end he had to be far away from all this beneficence!

Finally they ushered in the Sabbath with song and praise and then proceeded to their homes, said the prayer of Sanctification, broke the Sabbath loaf, ate the Sabbath feast, and drew the sanctity of the Sabbath into their very limbs. And many of the most precious folk of Jerusalem came to visit them, as people go to the Sabbath eve feast before a circumcision; since each person who goes up to the Land of Israel is like a new-born child, having taken upon himself the Covenant of the Land. So they sat all night long, reciting tales and legends and uttering song and praise, until the sun rose and they proceeded to the synagogue.

Having come to the synagogue, they prayed sweetly with full hearts. Who shall describe the great virtue of prayer in the Land of Israel, and all the more in Jerusalem, where once the Temple rose of which it is written, 'Mine eyes and My heart shall be there perpetually.'

Rabbi Shelomo went up twice to recite the priestly blessing, since in Jerusalem the priests raise their hands in blessing every day and not merely at festivals as is the practice throughout by far the greater part of the Exile; and on days when the Additional Prayer is said, they raise their hands in blessing both at the Morning and Additional Prayers. And Rabbi Shmuel Yosef, the son of Rabbi Shalom Mordekhai ha-Levi, poured water on the hands of the priests from a silver ewer which Rabbi Moshe had brought from the home of his grandfather, Rabbi Avigdor. Rabbi Shmuel Yosef used to fulfil with fervor every injunction which came his way and all the more so those which served as a commemoration of the Temple. While pouring the water, his hands trembled so for joy that the ewer beat against the basin and it gave forth a sound like the musical instruments of the Levites of old. The Priests went up to their platform, turned their faces to the people, parted their bent fingers on which the blessings are engraved, raised their hands on high, blessed the congregation in a voice like the voice of the wings of the cherubim in the Garden of Eden, and prolonged the blessings until the congregation had said the Thanksgiving, which they then closed with Amen. Great was the joy of Rabbi Shelomo, and great indeed the love with which he chanted his blessing when he first had the merit of going up to the priest's stage, to recite the blessing in Jerusalem, the Holy City. The blessings fairly tripped over themselves in their haste.

To the reading of the Torah they summoned Rabbi Shelomo first as Priest, after him Rabbi Shmuel Yosef as Levite, then Rabbi Pesah as third reader, followed by Rabbi Yosef Meir as fourth, by Rabbi Alter the teacher as fifth, Rabbi Alter the slaughterer as sixth, then Rabbi Yehudah Mendel as seventh, and Rabbi Moshe for the closing passage and the reading from the Prophets. Leibush the butcher was honored with the raising of the Torah on high for all the congregation to see, and the man whose name we have forgotten was honored with the rolling up of the Torah Scroll. They recited the blessings before and after the reading and also the blessing of thanks to God as befits seafarers who have come up from the sea. The congregation responded Amen after them, and wished them to be worthy to remain in the Palace of the King until such time as the Messiah King is revealed, may it be speedily and in our days. Amen.

All of a sudden a fine voice was heard, finer than all the voices there and like to that voice which we heard upon the sea. Our comrades looked up and saw Hananiah before them, his face bright with joy and radiant as the waves of the sea when the moon shines upon them. He was taller than he had been and wore shoes upon his feet. He greeted them and rejoiced with them exceedingly, saying, Sons of the living God, happy are you that you have come hither.

But who brought you up here? they asked him.

I spread my kerchief out upon the sea, he answered, and I sat upon it until I reached the Land of Israel.

Then they knew that the figure they had seen floating upon the sea had been Hananiah.

And they uttered praise and thanksgiving to the One

who is worthy of all praise, yet unto whom all praise is as nothing, and in whom all those who hope need never be shamed; as it is written, 'I am the Lord, for they shall not be ashamed that wait for me,' and they said, 'The Lord is good unto them that wait for Him.' And of Hananiah they said, 'But he that trusteth in the Lord, mercy compasseth him about.'

After the prayer the Holy Congregation of Jerusalem celebrated with a fine repast in their honor, with grape wine and brandy wine, which each man makes for himself at the time of the vintage shortly before the Feast of Booths. Householders from all over town sent them preserves of citron, of figs, and of other fine fruits for which the Land of Israel is famous; and they showed them every manner of affection. But above all they showed their affection for Hananiah, who had accepted the covenant of suffering and the Covenant of the Land. Indeed, they wished to place him at their head, but he belittled himself and took the lowest place next to the door. When our righteous Messiah comes, said he, we shall not be able to push too close to him, and then he will have to invite me higher up if he wants me. And then I shall know that I have some slight degree of importance as far as he is concerned. And if I have not, then who am I anyway to be seated at the head?

Thus they sat and drank of all the wines and many times blessed the One who is good and who does good, and they studied the passage dealing with the ten sanctities whereby the Land of Israel is sanctified more than all other lands. A vegetable was brought to our comrades which tasted like fowl fried in goose fat. How remarkable is the Land of Israel! Here is a vegetable

which you can buy in the market two for a penny. Take
and fry it in sesame oil, and it tastes like fowl fried in
goose fat. Then they said the grace for wine and food,
and washed their hands for the feast.

AFTER the Sabbath our comrades hired themselves a dwelling near the Western Wall,
the windows of which directly faced the site of the
Temple; and so they found themselves in the presence
of the Divine Presence. The women purchased themselves garments of white wool and the choicest food and
drink of the Land, and of its fruits. They cooked and
baked and conducted their households with wisdom.
They lacked for nothing, even having goat's milk for
the Feast of Weeks.

xiv
In the
presence
of the
Divine
Presence

Our comrades resided before the Lord in the Land of
Life, in Jerusalem, devoting themselves to Torah and
prayer and good deeds and the practice of charity, and
to love and to fear and to humility. And on the eve of
the New Moon and the other days on which the Prayers
of Supplication are said, they would go out to the Holy
Places and pray for themselves and their brethren in
exile.

All hours are not the same. It is widely known that
every righteous man who comes up from outside the
Land to the Land of Israel must begin by falling from
his original level. For the air of the Land of Israel is
holy and a reduction is necessary to precede Being. But
his Name, be blessed, came to their aid and gave them

the strength to accept submissively all that befell them, until they were worthy to receive a fresh intelligence, the intelligence of the Land of Israel. Day after day they were tried and tested, by insults and by curses, by loss of money and injury to their persons. For Jerusalem is not as the places that are outside the Land, since never has a man gone to sleep in Jerusalem bearing unrequited sins. For day after day the Holy One, blessed be he, settles that day's accounts, in order that the spiritual debts of Jerusalem might not increase and multiply. Like a judge of flesh and blood, who considers and reconsiders the cases of those brought before him that they might be found innocent; so the Holy One, blessed be he, turns, as one might say, his eyes on Jerusalem and chastises its inhabitants that they might be cleansed of every iniquity.

Pessel, the daughter of Rabbi Shelomo, perished from the kick of a mule, and Feiga perished from the blows of Ishmael. For once a water carrier brought water to Feiga on a day when it was raining heavily and all the cisterns and wells were full, so that she did not need his water. Thereupon he emptied his water-skins over her, and she caught a chill and died.

But our men of good heart lovingly accepted everything that befell them, not rebelling at their sufferings or making claims on the Divine Presence. Instead they bore with all their losses and comforted themselves, saying that on the morrow the Holy One, blessed be he, would redeem them and then all their troubles and distress would be over. And when the common people used to ask why the Holy One, blessed be he, did not exact vengeance upon the wicked nations who treated his children like captives, they would reply, Our answer is in the words of your question: Once there was a king whose son was attacked by enemies. Thereupon the king said, Why should I go to the trouble of sending soldiers to avenge myself on them? I shall immediately go forth myself with all my army to expel and sentence them for making my son suffer; and I shall bring my son back home with much joy and honor.

All trouble is hard to bear, but hardest of all is the trouble of making a living. When a man becomes poor, hunger irks him every day. There seemed to be a hole in our comrades' pockets and their money ran out. Before the end of the year they felt the hardships of making a living, since the Land of Israel has been purged of all vanities and there is no source of money save the money that a man brings with him from abroad. And so at length they were compelled to obtain their sustenance from the Exile.

When that time came, Leibush the butcher separated from the group and made up his mind to return to Buczacz. For Leibush said, Have you ever seen a country where nothing is to be had but mutton? From the very beginning he had not been pleased with Jerusalem. What he sought he did not find, while with what he did find his body was not satisfied. On the other hand, Rabbi Yosef Meir also had to prepare to leave. He wished to dwell in the Land of Israel but was not permitted to, on account of an ancient ordinance that no man may dwell in Jerusalem without a wife for more than a single year.

But the Holy One, blessed be he, will use one and the

same means for chastising the unrighteous and for doing good to the righteous. The ship on which Leibush returned to the Exile had brought with it the divorced wife of Rabbi Yosef Meir. On her arrival he sent her greetings and afterwards brought her under the bridal canopy, and Rabbi Yosef Meir lived to see a generation of upright, God-fearing and God-loving descendants. Rabbi Pesah and Tzirel were likewise found worthy in the course of their residence in the Holy City, and their house was builded by sons and by daughters who in due course of time were enlisted in the legions of the Lord of the Universe.

And so our redeemed brethren dwelled together within the Holy Congregation of the Holy City, joyously fulfilling the commandment to dwell in the Land of Israel; until their end came and they passed away, returning their souls unto Him to whom all souls belong, and leaving their bodies to the bosom of their mother; for they were found worthy to be buried in the soil of the Holy Land on the Mount of Olives at Jerusalem, facing the Temple of the Lord, at the feet of the Holy One, blessed be he; until the time comes for them to awaken to everlasting life, on the day of which it is written: 'And His feet shall stand in that day upon the mount of Olives.'

But Hananiah lived many long years, strength and energy accruing to him year by year. When he was a hundred years old, he was like a lad of twenty in his fulfilment of the commandments and performance of good deeds; and neither weakness nor weariness could be recognized in him. Many fanciful tales are told about that same Hananiah, such as the tale that when our men of

good heart arrived on shore at Jaffa, they found Hananiah drying his kerchief in the sun. But this is not the
truth, as Hananiah was already in Jerusalem ere his
comrades had arrived in the Land. All kinds of fanciful
tales are likewise told about his kerchief; for instance,
that the Emperor Napoleon saw it and made a flag out
of it and was victorious in his wars. But that is not the
truth either, since, when Hananiah had passed away,
they covered his eyes with his kerchief.

The day on which Hananiah died was the eve of the
month of Nisan. He had tied his kerchief round his
loins and was about to proceed to the synagogue. Suddenly he felt his legs failing. This fellow's legs, said he,
are entreating him not to bother them; so I shall pray
at home.

And when he came to the words, 'The heavens are the
heavens of the Lord; but the earth hath He given to the
sons of man,' his soul departed from him in purity.
They came and closed his eyes and covered them with
his kerchief. Then with much difficulty they took his
prayer book out of his hands, purified his body, and
brought him to his eternal home.

Many accompanied him to the cemetery, and many
spoke his praises. One praised him for his simplicity,
another for his whole-heartedness, a third for his nim-
bleness in fulfilling commandments, a fourth for his
love of the Land of Israel, a fifth for his faith, and a
sixth for all of these qualities together. For all the good
and upright qualities which were given to Israel to glor-
ify God's blessed world were to be found together in
Hananiah, peace be upon him.

The sages and rabbis of Jerusalem have long desired that all that befell Hananiah should be put on record in a book. But by reason of harshness of servitude and the urgency of livelihood, as well as because of strife and contention, the matter was deferred from day to day and from year to year; until I came and wrote all the adventures of Hananiah in a book which I have called 'In the Heart of the Seas.' This name I have given this book in memory of Hananiah, peace be upon him, who went down into the heart of the sea and came forth peacefully. I have not left out anything I have heard and I have added nothing more than my soul advised.

Some will read my book as a man reads legends, while others will read it and derive benefit for themselves. With regard to the former I quote the words of the Book of Proverbs: 'But a good word maketh the heart glad'; a good word maketh the soul to rejoice and delivereth from care. But of the latter I say in the words of the Psalmist: 'But those who wait for the Lord, they shall inherit the land.'

ASHKENAZI – *one 7 2 and 8 my t (see p. 90)*

ADAR: Hebrew month; February or March.

ALFASI: Isaac Alfasi (eleventh century), author of a famous Talmudic compilation.

BOOK OF SPLENDOR *(Zohar):* the chief work of the earliest Kabbalah (end of thirteenth century).

COUNTING OF OMER: see Leviticus 23:15.

DAY OF ATONEMENT *(Yom Kippur):* the tenth of the Days of Awe, which start with the New Year's Day; a day of prayer, fasting, and forgiveness of sins.

EIGHTEEN BENEDICTIONS: one of the oldest parts of the Jewish liturgy, occurring in the weekday prayer service.

FEAST OF BOOTHS: identical with Feast of Tabernacles; during this holiday Jews live in booths covered with leaves.

FEAST OF TABERNACLES *(Sukkot):* an eight-day holiday, beginning on the fifth day after the Day of Atonement. It commemorates the wandering of the Israelites in the desert.

FEAST OF WEEKS *(Shavuot):* a two-day holiday (in Israel, one day), seven weeks after Passover. It is a feast of first fruits and a season dedicated to the memory of the revelation on Mount Sinai.

GAON: *lit.,* excellence; title given to outstanding rabbis.

HAKHAM: wise man; scholar. Also, title given to a Sephardic rabbi.

HOSANNAH: "Save, I pray."

HOSANNAH WILLOWS: twigs of willow used in the synagogue on the Feast of Tabernacles.

HOUSE OF PRAYER: see House of Study.

HOUSE OF STUDY *(Bet ha-Midrash):* a place of learning and worship. Usually identical with the House of Prayer.

ISRAEL THE BAAL SHEM TOV ("Master of the Good Name"): founder of the Hasidic movement (eighteenth century).

IYAR: Hebrew month; April or May.

KABBALAH: *lit.,* tradition; Jewish mysticism; its writings pointed to the deeper layers of religion, which it represented as the authentic "tradition" of Israel.

KARAITE: member of a Jewish sect professing to follow the Bible to the exclusion of rabbinical tradition.

KETUVOT: Talmudic tractate, dealing with the marriage contract.

KOHEN ("priest"): descendent of Aaron.

LULAV: palm branch, used in the liturgy on the Feast of Tabernacles.

MEIR OF THE MIRACLE: Talmudic master of the second century C.E. Centuries later he came to be considered a miracle worker.

MEZUZAH: parchment scroll containing scriptural texts, attached to the door of a Jewish home.

MISHNAH: the earliest and basic part of the Talmud.

NISAN: Hebrew month; March or April.

ORDERED TABLE *(Shulhan Arukh):* code of Jewish law, compiled by Josef Karo (sixteenth century).

PASSOVER *(Pesah):* eight-day holiday (in Israel, seven days) occurring in the Spring and commemorating the exodus from Egypt.

PHYLACTERY *(tefillin):* leather cubicles containing scriptural texts inscribed on parchment. They are attached to the left arm and the head during the weekday morning service. They are a sign between God and Israel.

PURIM: the feast of "lots" (Esther 9:25); holiday commemorating the defeat of the wicked Haman; it is observed by the reading of the Book of Esther and by games and masquerades.

RABBI ABRAHAM IBN EZRA: outstanding Bible exegete, religious philosopher, and poet (twelfth century).

RABBI AKIBA: leading Talmudic master of the second century C.E.

RABBI HAYYIM BEN ATTAR: author of a commentary to the Pentateuch; settled in Jerusalem in 1742.

RABBI MEIR OF PRIMISHLAN: Hasidic master of the nineteenth century.

RABBI MOSHE BEN MAIMON: Moses Maimonides, foremost Jewish thinker and scholar (twelfth century).

RABBI SIMEON BAR YOHAI: Talmudic master of the second century.

RASHI (Rabbi Solomon ben Isaac): classical commentator (eleventh century) on the Bible and the Babylonian Talmud.

ROSH HA-SHANAH: New Year, occurring in the Fall; days of judgment.

SANHEDRIN: the high council in the time of the Second Temple. Also, a Talmudic tractate.

SHADDAI: one of the names of God.

SHEOL: netherworld.

TEHINNOT: private prayers and meditations, usually recited by women.

THE WAY OF LIFE *(Orah Hayyim):* first of the four parts of the Ordered Table.

YESHIVA: Talmudic academy.

ZADDIK ("the righteous one"): title given to the leader of a Hasidic community.